Egyptian Hieroglyphs

Cover Columns of painted hieroglyphs, part of a religious text. Fragment from the tomb of King Seti I, Valley of the Kings, Thebes. Nineteenth Dynasty, *c.* 1300 BC. H. 24 cm. BM 5610.

1 Limestone wall panel, decorated with figures and hieroglyphs, from the tomb of a man called Iry. Fifth Dynasty. H. 95 cm. BM 1168.

Egyptian Hieroglyphs

W. V. Davies

Published for the Trustees of the British Museum
by British Museum Press

Preface

The limitations of this book should be stated at the outset. It is simply too brief to do justice to a system of communication as complex and many-sided as the hieroglyphic writing of ancient Egypt. The account of the subject presented here has had to be very selective, covering, in an introductory manner, only those areas that I believe to be of the greatest importance and interest. For more detailed and scholarly treatments of the various aspects of the system, readers are recommended to consult the works listed in the Bibliography.

In the preparation of the book I have been kindly and ably assisted in various ways by a number of colleagues. Mr T. G. H. James made several valuable suggestions concerning its organization and content; Professor A. F. Shore and Miss Carol Andrews provided information on Coptic and demotic matters; Mrs Christine Barratt drew the line illustrations and the hieroglyphs in the text; Mr Peter Hayman prepared the bulk of the photographic material; Miss Felicity Jay typed the final copy; members of the staff of British Museum Publications skilfully expedited the book's completion and its progress through the press. To all these I offer grateful thanks, as I do also to those institutions who have allowed me to use illustrations of objects in their collections.

i'm Rhieni â diolch

Published by British Museum Press a
division of British Museum Publications Ltd
46 Bloomsbury Street, London WC1B 3QQ
Fifth impression 1992

Designed by Arthur Lockwood
Front cover design by Grahame Dudley

Set in Linotype 202 Sabon and printed at
The Bath Press, Avon

British Library Cataloguing in Publication Data
Davies, W. V.
Egyptian hieroglyphs.—(Reading the past)
1. Egyptian language—Writing, Hieroglyphic
I. Title. II. British Museum. III. Series
493'.1 PJ1097

ISBN 0-7141-8063-7

Contents

1
The Language

Ancient Egyptian occupies a special position among the languages of the world. It is not only one of the very oldest recorded languages (probably only Sumerian is older) but it also has a documented history longer by far than that of any other. It was first written down towards the end of the fourth millennium BC and thereafter remained in continuous recorded use down to about the eleventh century AD, a period of over 4,000 years. Egyptian, or Coptic (as the last stage of the language is called), expired as a spoken tongue during the Middle Ages, when it was superseded by Arabic. It is now, strictly, a dead language, though it continues to 'live on', albeit in a fossilised form, in the liturgy of the Coptic church in Egypt. Although it can only be a minute fraction of what was actually produced, the body of written material to have survived in Egyptian is, nevertheless, enormous. It consists, in large part, of religious and funerary texts, but it also includes secular documents of many different types – administrative, business, legal, literary and scientific – as well as private and official biographical and historical inscriptions. This record is our most important single source of evidence on ancient Egyptian society.

Since the decipherment of the writing system in the third decade of the last century (see Chapter 5), the language has been among the most thoroughly researched areas of Egyptology. As a result, although a great deal of vocabulary and many points of grammar remain to be fully elucidated, our understanding of the basic structure of Egyptian and of the rules governing its operation can now be considered to be on a reasonably firm footing. It is not only Egyptologists who have taken an interest in the language. In recent years increasing attention has been paid to Egyptian by linguists concerned with the study of human language as a general phenomenon. In this area, Egyptian is of particular importance to comparative and historical linguists, its longevity offering a rare opportunity for the testing of theories concerning the nature and rate of language change and development.

Egyptian is one of a group of African and Near Eastern languages (many of them still living tongues) which have sufficient similarities in their grammar and vocabulary to suggest that they are derived from a common linguistic ancestor. This group is known to scholars as Afro-Asiatic (or Hamito-Semitic). The Afro-Asiatic family is deemed at present to consist of six co-ordinate branches, of which Ancient Egyptian forms one. The other five are: Semitic (sub-branches of which include such well-known languages as Akkadian, Hebrew and Arabic), Berber (found in north Africa to the west of Egypt), Chadic (found in the sub-Saharan regions to the east, south and west of Lake Chad), Cushitic (found in the Sudan, Ethiopia, Somalia and north-west Kenya) and Omotic (found in southern Ethiopia). Of these, only Egyptian and Semitic are favoured with substantial written traditions; in the case of the others, written sources are minimal or even non-existent and a great deal of basic recording and analysis still remains to be achieved. There is as yet no consensus as to the date when the various branches separated from the proto-language. Recent estimates, based largely on the degree of differentiation between early Egyptian and Akkadian (the oldest recorded form of Semitic), vary widely. One scholar has placed the likely date of separation at around 6000 BC, another at around 12000 BC.

There is no evidence that the ancient Egyptians took a serious interest in the analysis of their own language. If works of grammar, such as those written in antiquity for Greek

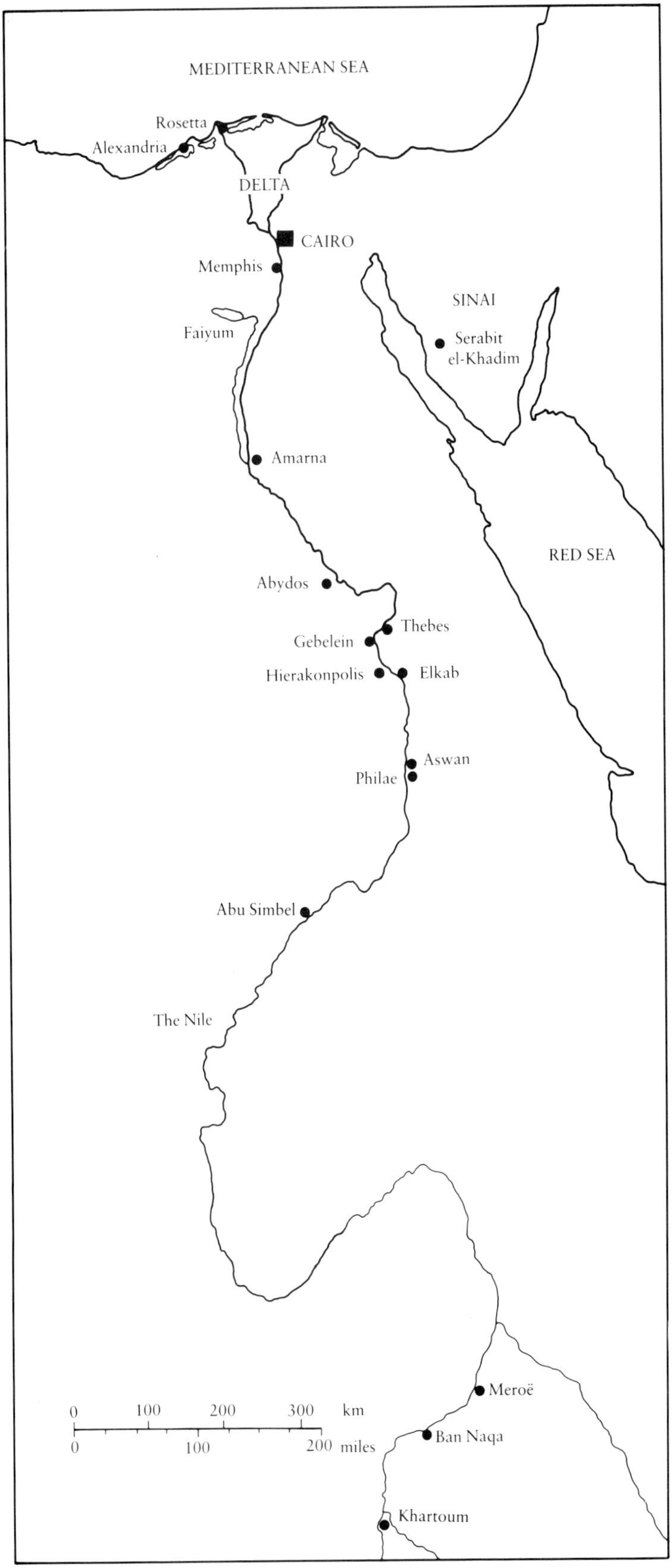

2 Egypt and the Sudan.

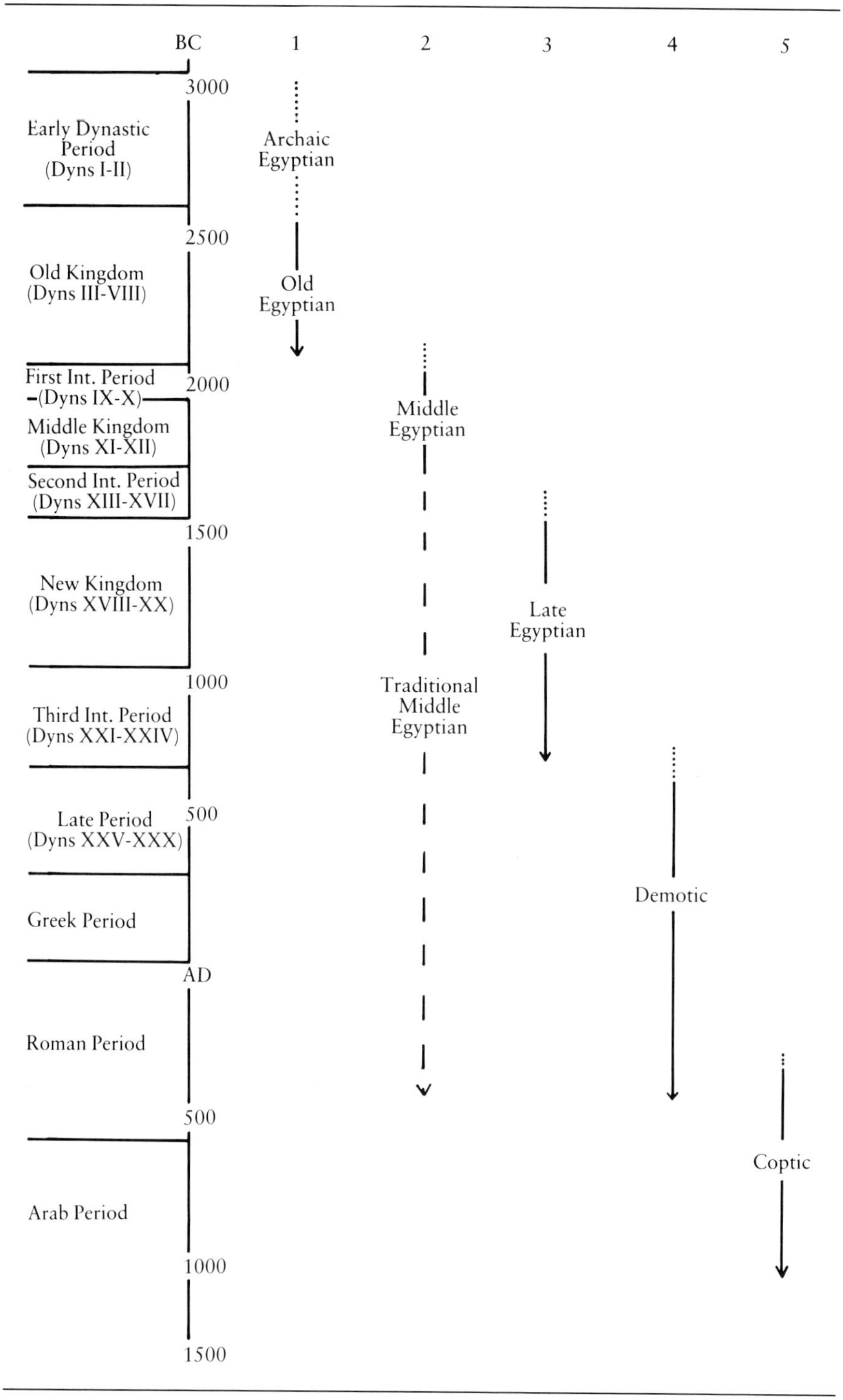

Table 1: Stages in the development of the Egyptian language.

and Latin, were composed for Egyptian, they have not survived. Our knowledge of Ancient Egyptian is entirely the product of modern scholarship. Egyptologists identify five, somewhat arbitrary, stages in the development of the language (see table opposite), each characterised by certain distinctive features of grammar and orthography, with the most fundamental point of division perceived as lying between the first two stages, on the one hand, and the last three, on the other. They have been arrived at by analysis and comparison of a large number of dated texts, covering the whole period of the recorded use of the language. Scholars, engaged in such work, have had always to keep in mind that the evidence at every stage consists of the language as *written*, and that written language rarely corresponds exactly to the spoken variety. Written language is more conservative: it frequently includes spellings that are partly or even wholly historical as well as words and grammatical constructions that have long ceased to be used in actual speech. Such redundancy is well evidenced in the case of Egyptian. In the following outline of the five stages it should be noted that the language of the very earliest inscriptions (from the late Predynastic and Early Dynastic Periods (*c.* 3100–2650 BC)), sometimes called 'Archaic Egyptian', is not included as a stage. This is because the inscriptions in question are too brief and limited in content to allow any meaningful analysis of the underlying language.

Old Egyptian
The language of the inscriptions of the Old Kingdom (*c.* 2650–2135 BC), the period in which the first continuous texts appear.

Middle Egyptian
The idiom, in particular, of the First Intermediate Period and the Middle Kingdom (*c.* 2135–1785 BC); regarded as the 'classical' stage of the language, used in literary, religious and monumental inscriptions through to the Graeco-Roman Period. Very close to Old Egyptian in structure.

Late Egyptian
The everyday language of the New Kingdom and Third Intermediate Period (*c.* 1550–700 BC), as witnessed particularly in secular documents of the Ramesside Period (*c.* 1300–1080 BC); also found to some extent in literary and monumental inscriptions. Very different from Old and Middle Egyptian, especially in its verbal structure.

Demotic
Vernacular successor of Late Egyptian, written in the script known as Demotic (see below, Chapter 2), attested from the beginning of the Late Period down to late Roman times (*c.* 700 BC—fifth century AD).

Coptic
The final stage of the language, as written in the Coptic script (see below, Chapter 2), from the third century AD onwards. The only stage of the language of which the vocalic structure is known and in which distinct dialects are recognisable. The two major dialects are: Sahidic, the standard literary dialect until the tenth century AD, its place of origin uncertain, possibly Thebes or Memphis; and Bohairic, originally the dialect of the west Delta, which supplanted Sahidic as the official dialect in the eleventh century.

2
The Scripts

By the Late Period of Egyptian history three distinct scripts were in use for writing the Egyptian language. They are known as hieroglyphic, hieratic and demotic respectively. They are superficially different from each other in appearance but actually represent the same writing system, hieratic and demotic being merely cursive derivatives of hieroglyphic. All three were eclipsed during the Roman Period by a fourth script, called Coptic, which was based on the Greek alphabet and operated on quite different principles. The present chapter will be devoted mainly to an account of some of the more important external features and conventions of the scripts; the principles underlying the native system will be dealt with in the next chapter.

Hieroglyphic

This was the earliest form of Egyptian script, and it was also the longest-lived. The first
36, 37 hieroglyphs appear in the late Predynastic Period, in the form of short label-texts on
stone and pottery objects from various sites, probably to be dated within the range
3 3100–3000 BC, while the last datable examples are to be found in a temple inscription
on the island of Philae carved in AD 394, nearly three and a half thousand years later. Originally the script was employed to write different kinds of texts, in a variety of media, but as its cursive version, hieratic, developed, hieroglyphic was increasingly confined to religious and monumental contexts, where it was rendered most typically in carved relief in stone. It was for this reason that the ancient Greeks called the individual elements of the script *ta hiera grammata*, 'the sacred letters', or *ta hieroglyphica*, 'the sacred carved (letters)', from which our terms 'hieroglyph' and 'hieroglyphic' are derived.

The signs of the hieroglyphic script are largely pictorial or 'iconic' in character. A few are of indeterminate form and origin, but most are recognisable pictures of natural or
man-made objects, which, when carefully executed, may exhibit fine detail and
cover colouring, although they are conventionalised in form and their colour is not always
realistic. There is little doubt that the best examples of the script have 'an intrinsic beauty of line and colour' that fully justifies the claim, often made, that 'Egyptian hieroglyphic writing is the most beautiful ever designed'. Its pictorial character should not, however, mislead one into thinking that the script is a kind of primitive 'picture-writing'. It is a full writing system, capable of communicating the same kinds of complex linguistic information as our own alphabet, though it does so by different means. Typologically the script is a 'mixed' system, which means that its constituents do not all perform the same function; some of the signs convey meaning, others convey sound (see Chapter 3).

The system was never limited to a fixed number of hieroglyphs. It contained a relatively stable core of standard signs throughout its history, but, in addition, new signs were invented as required, while others fell into disuse. Developments in material culture were influential in this process. Innovations in Egyptian weaponry at the beginning of the New Kingdom, for example, saw the introduction of hieroglyphs for the
4 horse and chariot, 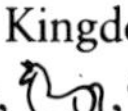, 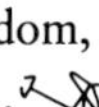, and for a new type of sword, 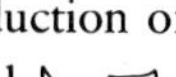. By the same process,
other hieroglyphs became obsolete and were either changed in form or entirely replaced; the sign for the royal *khepresh*-crown was 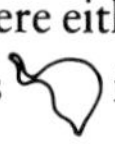 in the Thirteenth Dynasty and  in the

Eighteenth Dynasty; the sign for the common razor was in the Old Kingdom, in the Middle Kingdom, and finally in the New Kingdom. In these cases developments in fashion and technology produced corresponding changes in the script, each sign in turn depicting the current form of the actual object. There was no consistency in the process, however. Many hieroglyphs, even those in culture-sensitive categories, retained a more or less regular form; others changed temporarily and then reverted. The common hieroglyph depicting scribal equipment, for example, was written in the Old Kingdom, 'up-dated' to in the First Intermediate Period, and then changed back to the Old Kingdom form, which remained standard thereafter.

Taken over the whole period of the script's use, the total number of known hieroglyphs is huge; over 6,000 have so far been documented. The figure is misleading, however. The vast majority of these signs are found only on the temple walls of the Graeco-Roman Period, when, perhaps for special religious and esoteric reasons, the number of hieroglyphs was deliberately increased. In earlier periods the repertoire in standard use at any one time was always fewer than 1,000 (for example, about 700 are attested for the period covered by Middle Egyptian proper), and of these only a relatively small proportion occurs with real frequency.

3 *Left* Temple inscription carved in AD 394. These are the latest firmly dated hieroglyphs yet attested. They label a representation of a god, whom they name as 'Merul, son of Horus'. Temple of Philae.

4 *Right* Inscription in a tomb of the early New Kingdom including some of the very earliest examples of hieroglyphs representing the chariot and the horse. Elkab.

A hieroglyphic inscription is arranged either in columns or in horizontal lines, the
former being the more ancient arrangement. The sequence of signs is continuous. There
are no punctuation marks or spaces to indicate the divisions between words. Orientation is usually rightward, with the individual signs and the inscription of which they
form a part read from right to left, and with upper taking precedence over lower. It has
been suggested by one authority that this preference for rightward orientation is derived
from the fact that human beings are generally right-handed; quite simply, in producing a
text, 'the scribe began on the side where the hand that did the writing happened to be
situated'. Leftward orientation does also occur but as a rule only in certain contexts; it
was employed, for example, in inscriptions that accompany figures facing left, or to
5 provide balance or symmetry in a larger composition. Examples of horizontal and
columnar inscriptions orientated in both directions are given below. The direction of
writing is indicated as well as the order in which the signs are to be read. It will be seen

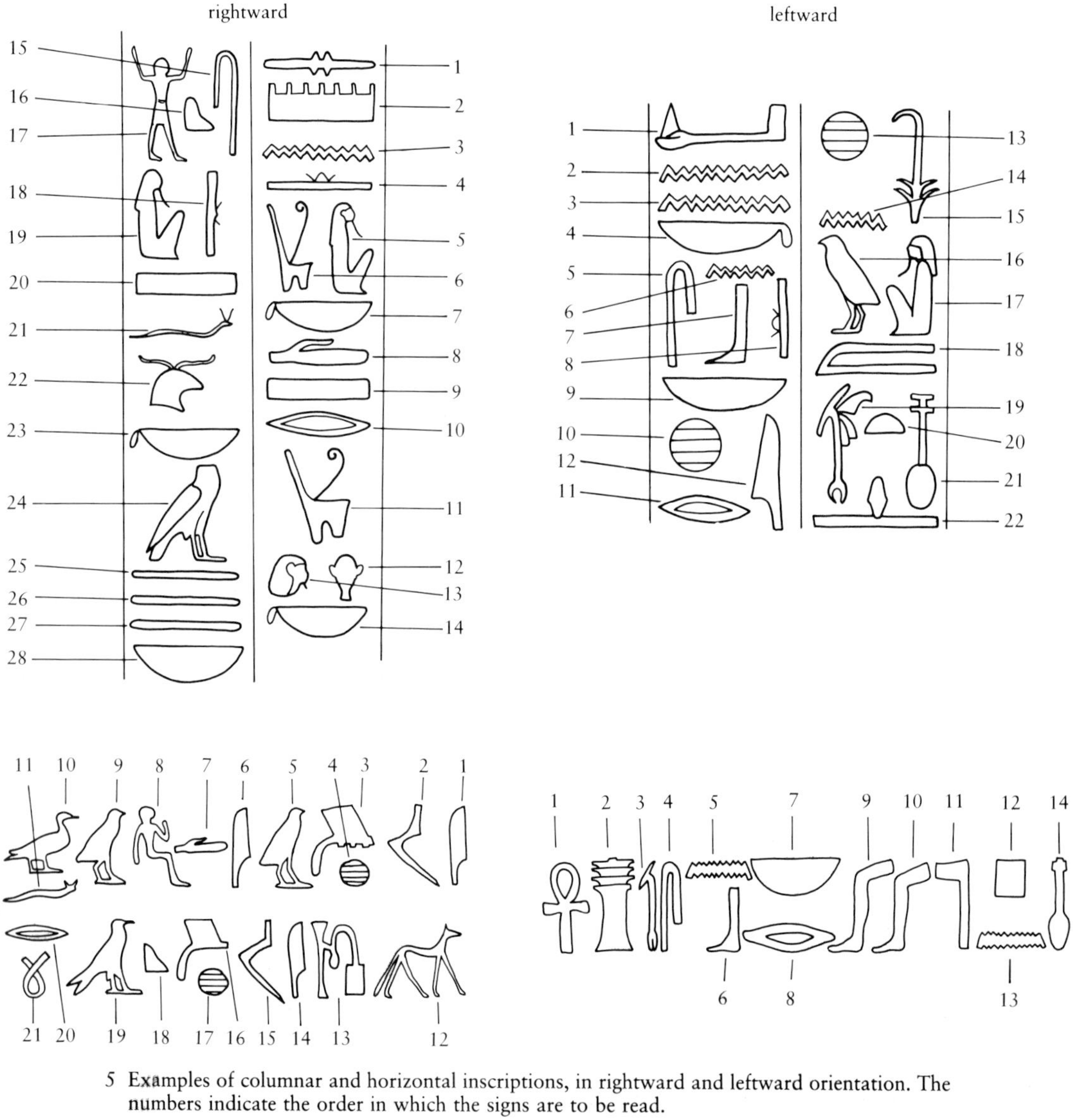

5 Examples of columnar and horizontal inscriptions, in rightward and leftward orientation. The numbers indicate the order in which the signs are to be read.

that a clue to the direction of reading is given by those signs, especially human or animal, that have a recognisable front and rear. Such signs in normal writing always face the beginning of the inscription.

Aesthetic or calligraphic considerations played a large part in the internal organisation of an inscription. Hieroglyphs were not written in linear sequence, one after another, like the letters of an alphabetic script, but were grouped into imaginary squares or rectangles so as to ensure the most harmonious arrangement and to minimise the possibility of unsightly gaps. Such requirements affected the relative size and proportions of individual signs and determined whether a word was written in full or in an abbreviated form. It is not uncommon to find hieroglyphs switched in their order for reasons of better spacing. Indeed 'graphic transposition', as it is called, is virtually the 6
rule for some sign combinations, particularly those in which a bird hieroglyph is written next to a small squat sign or a tall thin one. Many such transpositions were initially designed to make the most effective use of space in columnar inscriptions, but became so standard that they were often retained in horizontal texts as well.

Sign order was similarly affected by considerations of prestige. Words for entities of high status (such as 'king', 'god', and the names of specific gods) were usually given precedence in writing over words which, in speech, they followed. Typical examples

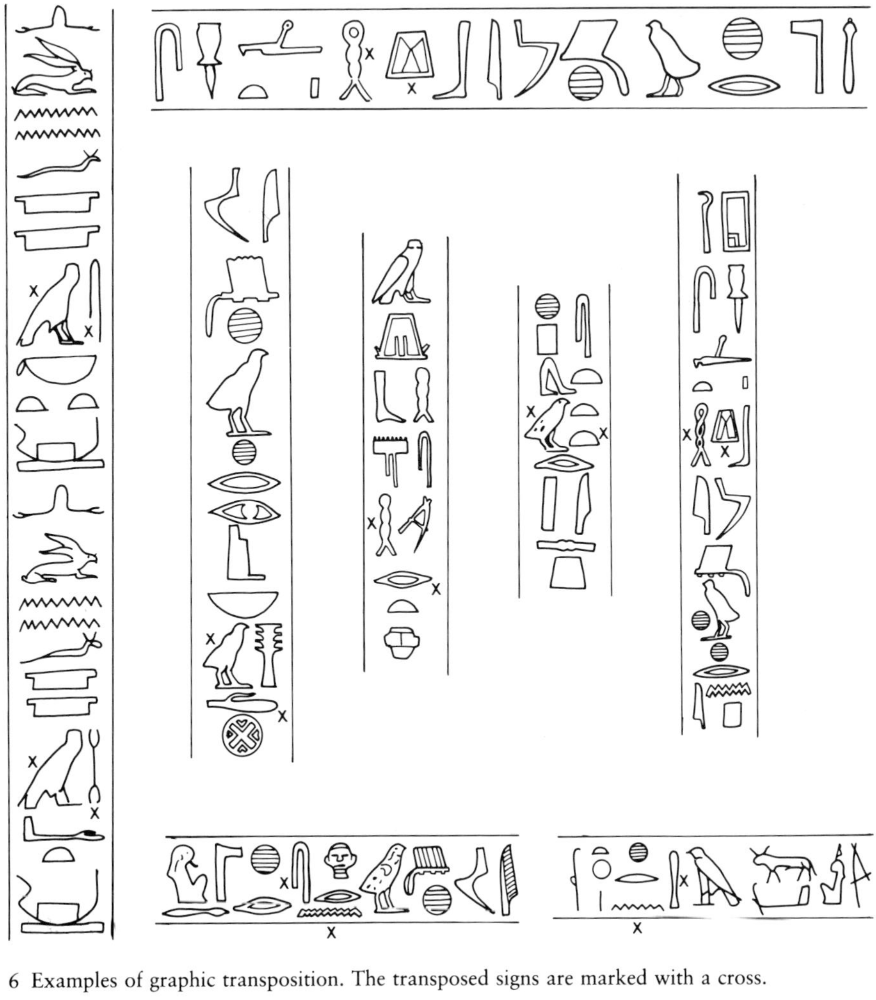

6 Examples of graphic transposition. The transposed signs are marked with a cross.

occur in the lines of an inscription on a tomb panel belonging to a man called Iry (written
1, 7). The first three signs of the inscription form the beginning of a common funerary formula which translates as 'An offering which Anubis gives'. In the order of signs the jackal hieroglyph occupies initial position in the group, whereas the word it represents, 'Anubis', actually comes third in the order of Egyptian speech. The jackal takes precedence because Anubis is a god. Similarly in the group , which is a title meaning 'priest of the king', the hieroglyphs for 'king', , are written before the hieroglyph for 'priest', , in reversal again of the actual word order. Graphic reversals of this kind are referred to as 'honorific transposition'.

The hieroglyphic script was always more than just a writing system. The Egyptians referred to it as , 'writing of the divine words', or simply as , 'divine words'. The individual hieroglyph was termed , 'sign', 'image', 'form', the same word as was sometimes used to denote a representation in Egyptian art. This terminology reflects two points of fundamental importance about the script: it was closely related to representational art and, like the art, it was endowed with religious or magico-religious significance.

The interrelationship between art and writing, which can be seen already on some of
36 the earliest inscribed monuments, is evident in a number of ways. Most obviously the hieroglyphs are themselves miniature pictures. In fact, in all essentials, they are small-scale versions of the larger 'actors' in an artistic scene. It is important to remember that Egyptian art was not a free form. It had a distinct purpose: to 'make to live' for eternity the things it depicted. In keeping with its purpose it was governed by strict rules as to content and manner of representation. A basic convention was that a figure should be depicted as objectively as possible, with no account taken of the effects of visual distortion. A figure was reproduced, two-dimensionally, in what was deemed to be its most 'characteristic' aspect; in the case of a complex figure, it might be necessary to embody more than one aspect in a single representation. The hieroglyphs follow this convention. Three instances, again from the inscriptions of Iry, may be taken to illustrate the point.
7 The sign below the jackal is a single hieroglyph with two parts. The lower rectangular part is a reed mat; the conical object centred above it is a loaf of bread. It is actually a picture of a loaf standing on a mat. The two are depicted, however, from different 'characteristic' view points. The loaf is shown in profile, the mat as if seen from above.
8 The same combination of views is apparent in the hieroglyph depicting items of scribal equipment. Side views are given of the narrow brush-holder and the round pigment bag, but a top view is shown of the rectangular palette with its characteristic paint-holes.
9 Even more illustrative is a third hieroglyph, representing an old man leaning on a stick. It is a very skilful carving, showing fine naturalistic detail, but it is not an organic whole. Close inspection will show that the figure is a composite, with the major parts of the body shown from different points of view. The head, the front breast, the arms and the legs are in profile view; the eye, the shoulders, and the rear breast in frontal; and the navel in three quarters. It is a picture of the body that combines in a single figure as many as possible of its essential aspects. The same diagrammatic approach informs the figures of Iry and his retinue on the same monument. It is the standard manner of representing the human body in Egyptian two-dimensional art.

The relationship between the figures and the hieroglyphs in the scene is not only a matter of internal structure. Each of the human figures has a separate inscription of its own, which identifies it by name and sometimes by title as well. The largest of the figures is identified as 'Priest of the king, Iry'. The smaller figure immediately in front of Iry is described as the 'scribe, Kai-nefer', the one behind as 'Iry-nedjes'. The three others

7 Panel of Iry. Detail of horizontal inscriptions at the top.

8 Panel of Iry. Detail of hieroglyph representing scribal equipment. H. 6.6 cm.

9 Panel of Iry. Detail of hieroglyph representing an old man. H. 9.2 cm.

10 Limestone statuette of Min-nefret; view showing inscription on the right side. Fourth Dynasty. H. 47 cm. BM 65430.

11 *Left* Limestone stela of Wennekhu and his son Penpakhenty, the names in each case followed by a 'name determinative' (). Nineteenth Dynasty. H. 35.3 cm. BM 1248.

12 *Above* Granite squatting figure of Sennefer. Such statues, because of their peculiar 'block' form, came to be regarded as suitable vehicles for long texts. Eighteenth Dynasty. H. 83.8 cm. BM 48.

shown facing the tomb owner are, from top to bottom, 'Nen-kai', 'Nefer-seshem-nesut' and 'Itjeh' respectively. In each case the writing follows in general the direction of the figure to which it belongs – rightward in the case of Iry, Iry-nedjes and Kai-nefer, leftward in that of the others. This correlation leads to a further point of identity. When a name occurs in an Egyptian inscription it is normally followed by a hieroglyph in the form of a male or female figure, called by Egyptologists a 'name determinative'. Its function is quite simply to clarify whether the name is that of a man or woman. In this case every one of the names lacks a small-scale determinative. The reason for this is that the larger figures, because of their proximity to the names, themselves act as determinatives. In other words, they function as large-scale hieroglyphs.

This kind of interdependence is not confined to two dimensions. The statue of the lady Min-nefret shows the same principle at work in three dimensions. The statue is 10
inscribed with hieroglyphs on the right and left sides of the seat. On each side the hieroglyphs are orientated in accordance with the figure. On the natural right side, they face rightwards; on the natural left, leftwards. The inscription ends with the lady's title and name, , 'the confidante of the king, Min-nefret'. Again there is no determinative, in this case because the statue serves as the determinative; it is actually here a three-dimensional hieroglyph.

The panel of Iry and the statue of Min-nefret both date to the Old Kingdom. This is the period when the relationship between art and writing is most consistently in evidence. The relationship remained in existence throughout the whole of Egyptian history but, after the Old Kingdom, a partial 'disengagement' gradually took place. Certain rules, such as those concerning orientation, continued to be observed, but there was an increasing tendency for the inscription on a monument to be treated as an entity in its own right. The virtual unity of name and figure was still sometimes respected on monuments as late as the New Kingdom, but more often than not it was disregarded and name 11
determinatives were appended even when a figure of the name's owner was depicted nearby. At the same time texts began to 'take over' the statues on which they were inscribed. Whereas in the Old Kingdom inscriptions were appropriately situated, on the seat or the pedestal of a statue, from the Middle Kingdom onwards they intrude, inorganically, on to the dress of the owner and eventually on to the body itself. The impression is, in the case of certain statues, that the figure has been viewed as primarily a 12
vehicle for the text that it bears.

As an integral part of a system of recreative art the hieroglyphs were naturally believed to have the power to bring to life what they depicted or stated. A funerary formula invoking benefits from a god was enough in itself, if written in hieroglyphs, to ensure the reception of those benefits by the deceased owner, as long as the owner was named, as in the case of Iry. The name of a person, inscribed in hieroglyphs, was believed to embody that person's unique identity. If the representation of a person lacked a name, it lacked also the means to ensure his continued existence in the after-life. To destroy the name(s) of a person was to deprive him of his identity and render him non-existent. On several occasions in Egyptian history the cartouches (name rings) of a dead ruler were systematically mutilated or removed from monuments on the orders of a vengeful 13
successor. Even the gods were not immune from such attack. When King Akhenaten sought, in the late Eighteenth Dynasty, to institute a new religion of the sun disk and abolish the old regime, he ordered, among other things, that the name of the existing chief of the gods, Amun, be removed from the monuments of the land, with effects that can still be seen on many surviving pieces. By similar means the monument of one person was often appropriated for the use of another. The essential act in such 'usurpation' was the change of name. The name of the original owner was removed; the name of the new

13 Detail of a basalt statue of a man holding a shrine. The hieroglyphic inscriptions include the cartouches of King Amasis deliberately effaced. Twenty-sixth Dynasty. H. of shrine 27 cm. BM 134.

14 Red granite statue of King Amenophis II of the Eighteenth Dynasty with inscriptions added by kings of the Nineteenth Dynasty. H. 2.6 m. BM 61.

one added; the monument might otherwise be left untouched. A statue of a king in the 14
British Museum provides a good example. On grounds of style and iconography it can be
identified as a portrait of Amenophis II of the Eighteenth Dynasty (*c.* 1400–1350 BC).
The cartouches it bears, however, are those of Ramesses II and Merenptah of the Nineteenth Dynasty (*c.* 1290–1200 BC). The statue was usurped for these later kings simply
by adding their names; no attempt was made to change the appearance of the piece to
make it conform to the style of their time.

Belief in the magical efficacy of the 'divine words' found further expression in the attempts that were occasionally made to limit the power of certain hieroglyphs, especially those depicting humans, birds and animals. These were deemed to have considerable potential for harm when located in magically 'sensitive' areas, like the walls of a burial chamber or the sides of a sarcophagus. The fear was that they might assume an independent hostile life of their own and consume the food offerings intended for the deceased or even attack the dead body itself. Steps were therefore taken to neutralise the danger that they posed. Sometimes such hieroglyphs were simply suppressed and replaced by anodyne substitutes. On other occasions they were modified in some way to immobilise
them. The bodies of human figures and the heads of insects and snakes were omitted, the
bodies of birds truncated, the bodies of certain animals severed in two, and the tails of 15
snakes abbreviated. Particularly dangerous creatures, such as the evil serpent, called
Apophis, the great enemy of the sun-god Rēʿ, were sometimes shown as constrained or
'killed' by knives or spears.

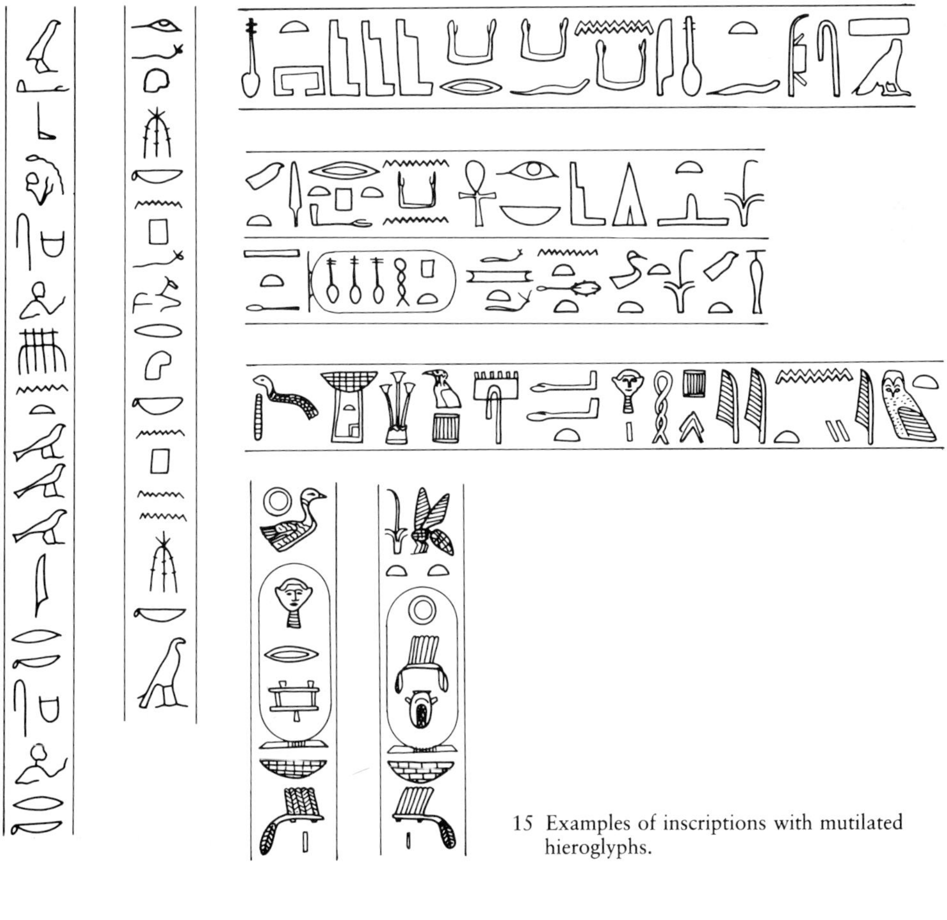

15 Examples of inscriptions with mutilated hieroglyphs.

Other hieroglyphs were regarded as having beneficial properties and were rendered in
three dimensions to serve as amulets or charms. When worn on the body these amulets
were believed to confer 'good luck' on their owners, whether living or dead. The amulet
16 in the form of the *sa*-sign, meaning 'protection', was one of several that offered protection against the powers of evil; the so-called *udjat*-eye of the god Horus was another.
17 The *ankh*- and the *djed*-signs offered the benefits of 'life' and 'endurance' respectively,
18, 19 while the hand, leg and face, and others like them, helped to restore the functions of the
19 bodily parts after death. The sign meaning 'horizon' shows the sun rising over a
mountain. It allowed the deceased to witness and identify with the sun's daily rebirth
and thereby be reborn himself.

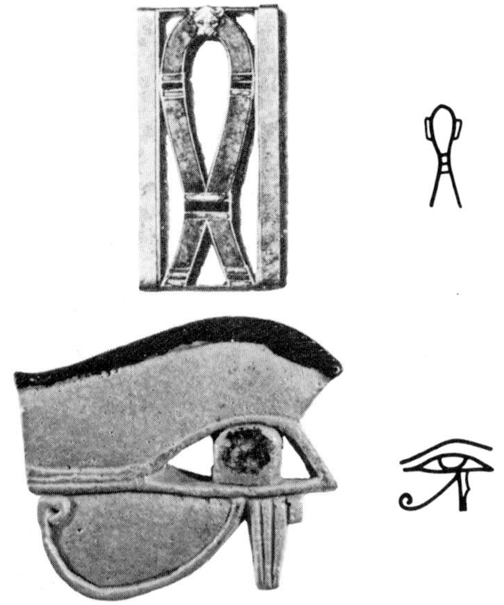

16–19 Amulets in the form of hieroglyphs.
16 *sa* (H. 3.9 cm, Cairo Museum, CG 52044, gold and semi-precious stones), *udjat* (H. 4.9 cm, BM 23092, faience).

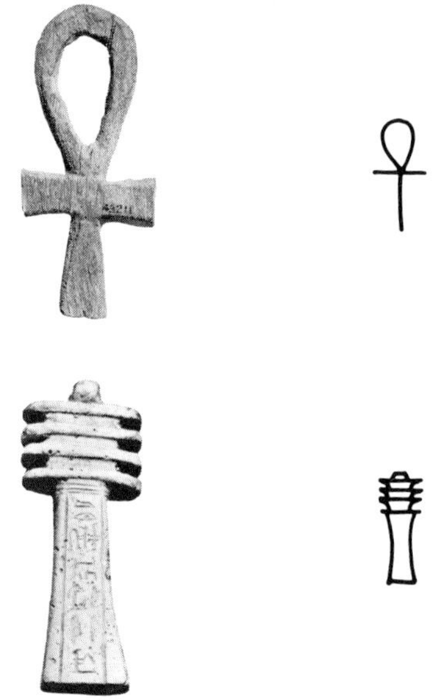

17 *ankh* (H. 11 cm, BM 43211, wood), *djed* (H. 7.4 cm, BM 50742, faience).

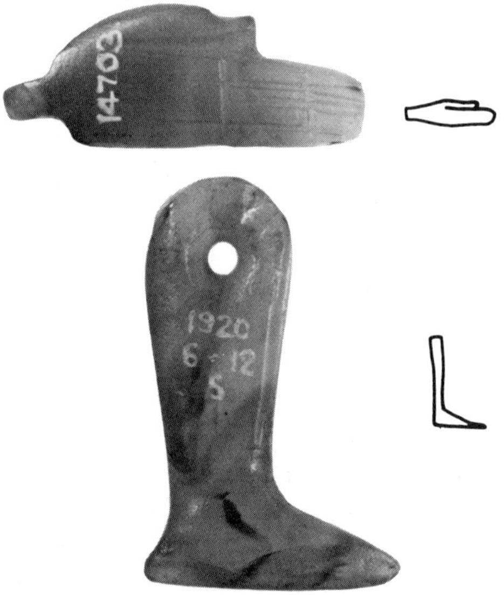

18 hand H. 0.7 cm, BM 14703, carnelian), leg (H. 1.9 cm, BM 54747, carnelian).

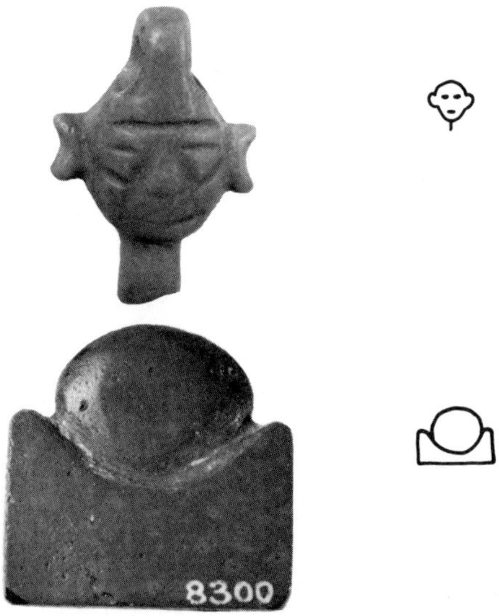

19 face (H. 1.7 cm, BM 57812, steatite), horizon (H. 2 cm, BM 8300, glass).

Hieratic

Hieratic is an adaptation of the hieroglyphic script, the signs being simplified to facilitate quick reproduction of a kind required in non-monumental contexts. It was Egypt's administrative and business script throughout most of its history, and was also employed to record documents of a literary, scientific and religious nature. It is found on all sorts of media, but most typically on rolls or sheets of papyrus or on bits of pottery and stone called ostraca. Documents in hieratic were usually written in black ink, applied by means of
20,21 a brush made out of a stem of rush. Red ink was occasionally employed to mark out a special section, like the beginning of a text or a numerical total, or to indicate punctuation points in literary compositions. There are also monumental examples where the script was incised in stone, but these are quite rare and of a relatively late date.

The earliest substantial body of texts in hieratic yet attested are estate records of the Fourth Dynasty, although sporadic examples of the script are known from much earlier. Its origin clearly goes back to the very beginning of writing in Egypt, since the first stages in its development are observable in the
37 semi-cursive hieroglyphs that occur as labels on vessels of the late Predynastic Period. The 'day-to-day' script of Egypt for nearly two and a half millennia, hieratic was finally ousted from secular use by another cursive script, demotic, at the beginning of the Late Period (*c.* 600 BC). Thereafter its use was confined to religious documents, which is why it was called *hieratika*, 'priestly', by the Greeks. The latest known hieratic documents are religious papyri dated to the third century AD. Like hieroglyphic, hieratic could be written either in columns or in horizontal lines but, unlike hieroglyphic, its orientation was invariable. Hieratic proper always reads from right to left. This is one of the features that distinguishes it from 'cursive hieroglyph', a script that resembles early hieratic and was the preferred form, for example, for reproducing certain kinds of funerary text (such as the Coffin Texts and
22 the 'Book of the Dead') from the Middle Kingdom down to the Third Intermediate Period.

20 *Right* Scribe's palette of ivory. It has two holes, one for black ink, one for red, and a slot for holding brushes. On the bottom are scribal jottings in hieratic. Eighteenth Dynasty. H. 30 cm. BM 5524.

21 *Below* Scene from a tomb painting showing a scribe conducting a census of geese. He stands reading from an unrolled papyrus with his palette tucked under his arm. Thebes. Eighteenth Dynasty. H. of scribe's figure 33.4 cm. BM 37978.

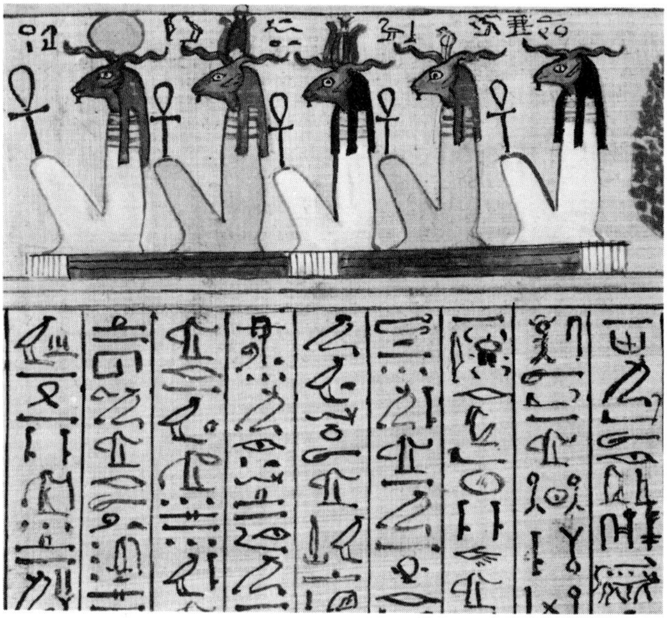

22 Cursive hieroglyphs in a 'Book of the Dead' of the Nineteenth Dynasty. The hieroglyphs accompanying the deities at the top are in leftward orientation. Those in the main text below are in rightward orientation. Papyrus of Hunefer. BM 9901,8.

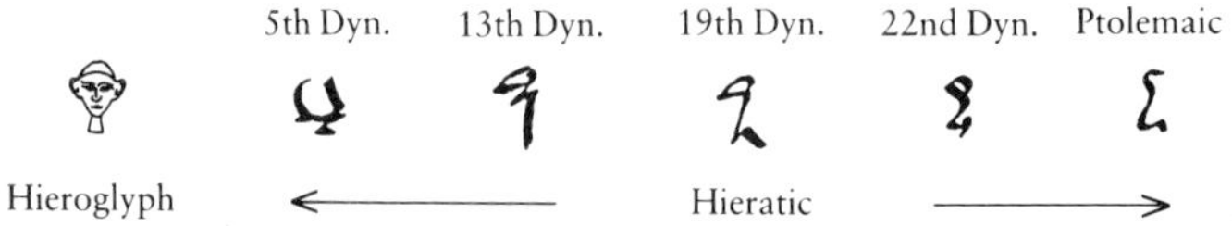

23 Cursive development.

24 Two common ligatures.

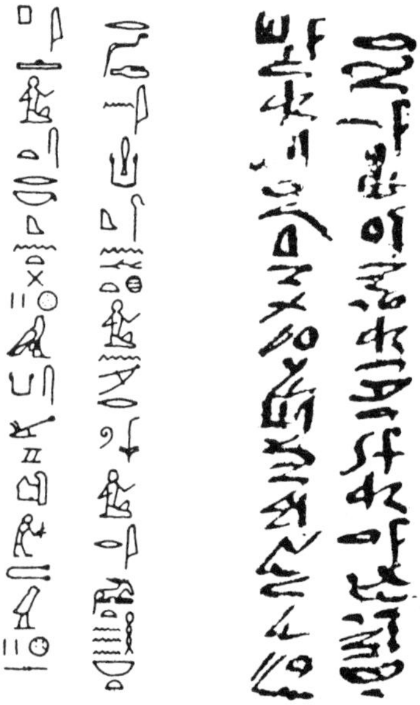

25 Section from a private letter in the hieratic script, written in columns on papyrus. Eleventh Dynasty. New York, Metropolitan Museum of Art.

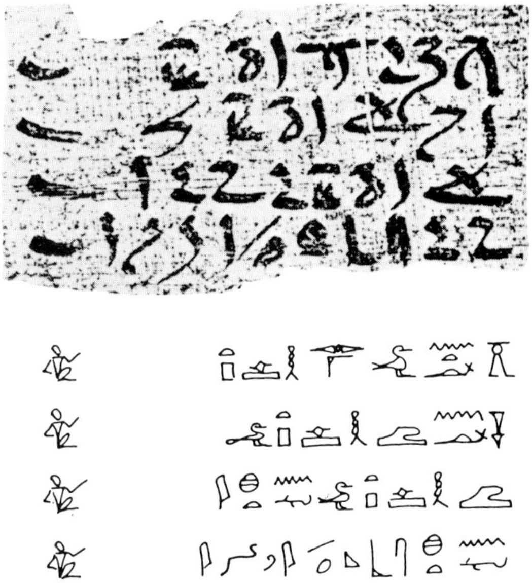

26 Part of an inventory of names written in the hieratic script, in horizontal lines. Twelfth Dynasty. Papyrus Reisner I. Boston, Museum of Fine Arts.

It is probably true to say that hieratic never completely lost touch with its monumental parent. It is always possible, with varying degrees of ease or difficulty, depending
on the period and type of inscription, to transcribe a hieratic text sign by sign into its
hieroglyphic equivalent. However, it followed its own course of evolution, the signs
showing a definite tendency to become progressively more cursive, and it also developed 23
other conventions and features appropriate to a running hand. Certain groups of two or
more signs came to be rendered by one stroke of the brush in what are called 'ligatures', 24
and complicated signs were often avoided or replaced by simple substitutes (for
example, the bird  was abbreviated to ) – these in turn were sometimes borrowed by
the hieroglyphic script, a reverse influence that is hardly surprising when it is considered
that in all probability many hieroglyphic inscriptions were initially drafted in hieratic.

A crucial period in the history of hieratic was the Middle Kingdom. Up to the Eleventh
Dynasty hieratic texts were usually written in columns. For some reason during the 25
Twelfth Dynasty there was a major change in practice. Scribes began to write in horizon- 26
tal lines, a mode that soon became universal. At the same time different styles of script
began to appear, which developed along their own lines. By the New Kingdom they had
become quite separate. One was a cursive 'business' hand used for writing mundane
documents, the other an elegant 'book' hand employed for literary texts and in contexts 27
where a 'traditional' hand was thought more appropriate. Out of the business hand of
the late New Kingdom there developed in turn, during the Third Intermediate Period,
two regional variants, both even more cursive – the so-called 'abnormal' hieratic in 28
Upper Egypt and demotic in Lower Egypt. Abnormal hieratic was completely supplanted by demotic in the Twenty-sixth Dynasty, following the conquest of the south by
kings of the north.

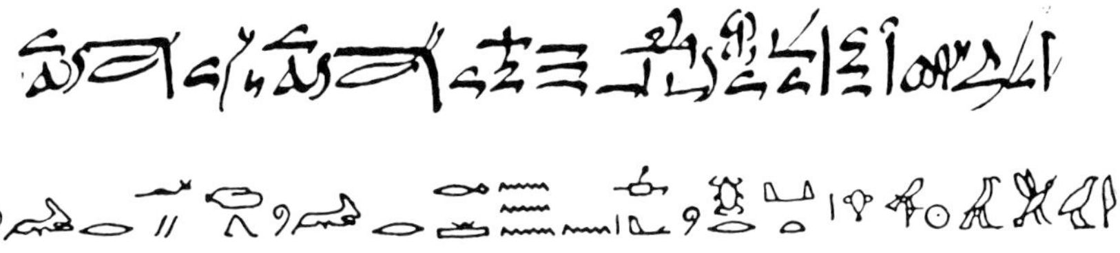

27 Line from a literary text. Nineteenth Dynasty. Papyrus d'Orbiney. BM 10183,3.

28 Papyrus with witness subscriptions in traditional hieratic (above) and abnormal hieratic (below). Twenty-sixth Dynasty. Papyrus Brooklyn 47.218.3. New York, The Brooklyn Museum.

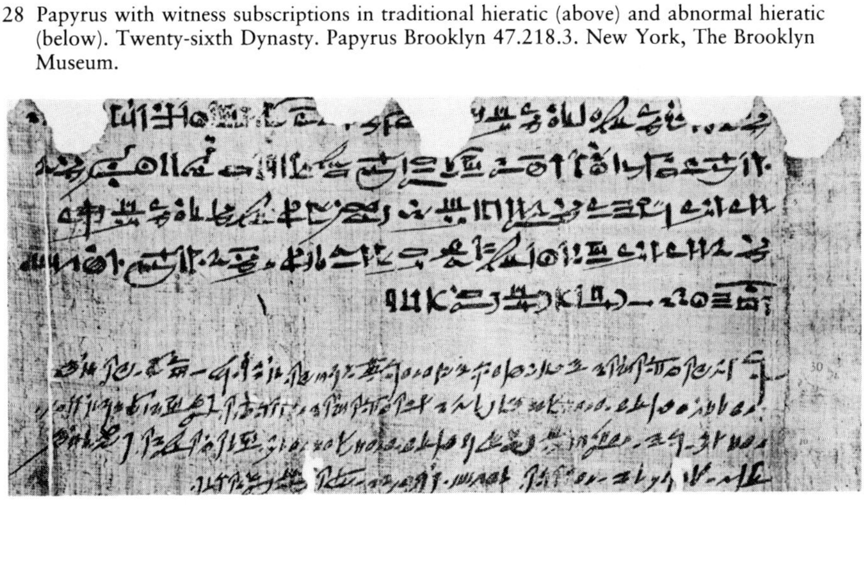

Demotic

For the rest of Egyptian history demotic was the only native script in general use for
day-to-day purposes. The name demotic, ancient Greek *demotika*, 'popular (script)',
refers to its secular functions, as does its Egyptian name *sẖ šʿt*, 'the writing of letters'.
29 Like hieratic, demotic was mostly confined to use on papyri and ostraca and it main-
tained the scribal tradition of writing in horizontal lines with rightward orientation.
It is otherwise an almost independent form, barely recognisable as a descendant of
hieratic, let alone hieroglyphic. It is a very cursive script, almost wholly lacking in icon-
icity and replete with ligatures, abbreviations and other orthographic peculiarities,
making it difficult to read and virtually impossible to transcribe meaningfully into any
kind of hieroglyphic 'original'.

The demotic record is dominated by legal, administrative and commercial material.
However, it also includes, from the Ptolemaic Period on, literary compositions, as well
as scientific and even religious texts, which were written in a more calligraphic hand, the
30 ink now increasingly applied with the reed pen introduced by the Greeks, which by the
end of the period had virtually supplanted the traditional brush. Another development
of the Ptolemaic Period was that the script began to be used monumentally, particularly
on funerary and commemorative stelae. The best-known example is the so-called
39 Rosetta Stone (see Chapter 5), which contains a single text, a priestly decree, repeated in
three scripts, hieroglyphic, demotic and Greek (the latter included as Greek was now the
official language of Egypt). All three versions, including the demotic, are incised in the
stone. Present evidence suggests that demotic outlived the two other native scripts by a
century or so before finally falling into disuse in the fifth century AD. The latest demotic
inscription is a graffito in the temple of Philae dated to AD 450.

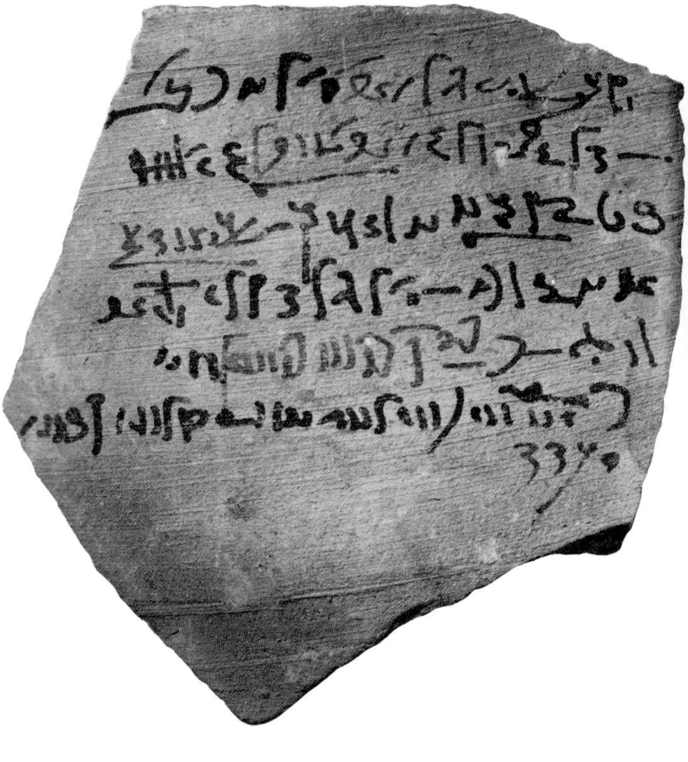

29 *Right* Demotic ostracon: a receipt for the delivery of wine in year ten of the Emperor Antoninus Pius. AD 145. H. 8.7 cm. BM 21426.

30 *Below* The reed pen introduced into Egypt by the Greeks. Traces of black ink survive on the tip of this example. Behnasa. 2nd century AD. L. 17.3 cm. BM 38145.

Coptic

As the old native scripts went into decline and finally disappeared during Egypt's Roman and Christian period, so a new script, Coptic, as used by the 'Copts', took their place to write the Egyptian language. The name 'Copt' is derived from the Arabic *gubti*, itself a corruption of the Greek *Aiguptios*. It means simply 'Egyptian'. It was the term used by the Arabs after their conquest of Egypt in the seventh century, to denote the native inhabitants of the country. Coptic represents a distinct departure from the other scripts. It consists of the twenty-four letters of the Greek alphabet, supplemented, in its standard, Sahidic, form, by six characters taken from demotic to denote Egyptian phonemes not known to Greek. It is thus a fully alphabetic script in which the vowels of the

31 Egyptian magical papyrus written in Greek and demotic letters. Behnasa. 2nd century AD. H. 29 cm. BM 10808.

language are represented, as well as the consonants. The letters borrowed from demotic and their phonemic values are as follows:

Demotic	Coptic	Value
	ϣ	sh
	ϥ	f
	ϩ	h
	ϫ	j
	ϭ	g
	ϯ	ti

The development of this standard form of the alphabet, which was well established by the fourth century AD, is closely associated with the spread of Christianity in Egypt. It has been suggested that the impetus for its development was provided by the need to furnish translations of the New Testament and other religious texts for the native population in a regularised and easily accessible form, a task for which the demotic script appears to have been considered both inadequate and inappropriate. The Coptic script was not, however, initially devised for Christian purposes. The earliest recognisable form of Coptic (datable to the end of the first century AD) was used to write native
31 magical texts, where the motive for the use of the Greek letters probably lay, it is thought, in the desire to render as accurately as possible the correct pronunciation of the magical 'words of power'. In 'Old Coptic', as it is called, the Greek letters are supplemented by several more demotic characters than are retained in the later standardised form of the script.

The surviving literature in Coptic is extensive, with a huge quantity, coming mostly from the libraries of monasteries, being devoted to religious, mainly Biblical, subjects. Non-religious material, much of it again originating from monastic communities,
32 includes private and official correspondence and administrative, business and legal documents, but very little of a purely 'literary' or scientific nature. Most of the surviving texts were written in ink, again with the reed pen, on papyrus or ostraca, though wooden tablets, parchment and, later, paper were also utilised, and the script was adapted
33 without difficulty for monumental use. Many of the documents are in the form of the 'codex', the ancestor of the modern book, made up of individual leaves of papyrus or

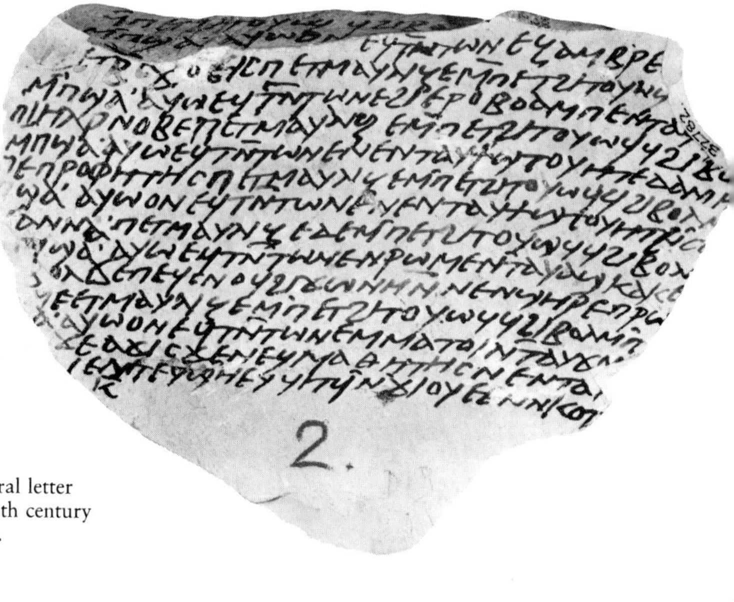

32 Coptic ostracon: a pastoral letter from a bishop. Thebes. 6th century AD. H. 13 cm. BM 32782.

33 Wooden lintel from a Coptic church with (left) invocation to 'The Lord Jesus Christ' for the blessed Jōkim and his wife. The damaged text on the right bears the date AD 914. L. 1.93 m. BM 54040.

parchment connected at the spine, which was introduced during the early centuries AD. Whatever the text or format the arrangement and direction of Coptic writing follow the common Greek mode. It is written or carved in horizontal lines reading from left to right. No gaps were left between words and punctuation was minimal (if present at all). A feature peculiar to Sahidic Coptic was the use of a superlinear stroke, unknown to Greek, which was regularly placed above certain consonants or groups of consonants to indicate a syllable.

Literacy

Although it is clear from the quantity and range of the extant record that writing played an immensely important part in ancient Egyptian society, it is very unlikely that literacy can have been widespread among the population. The production of writing, and direct access to it, was almost certainly the preserve of an educated élite, consisting, at the highest level, of royalty and high officials of state and, below them, of people for whom the ability to read and write was a necessary part of their job. There is no doubt that the routine exercise of literacy was largely a function of the professional scribe, who was a 21 central figure in every aspect of the country's administration – civil, military and religious.

Recent estimates, admitted to be no more than informed guesses, suggest that less than 1 per cent of the population would have been literate during most of the Pharaonic Period, rising to about 10 per cent in the Graeco-Roman Period, when Greek was the official language of Egypt. Within this generality, allowance must, of course, be made for considerable local variation deriving from special circumstances, such as existed, for example, in the village of Deir el-Medina, the home of the community of workmen who built and decorated the royal tombs at Thebes during the New Kingdom. Draughtsmanship and writing played such an important part in the daily work of these men that they were probably significantly more literate than the general populace. Among the latter, literacy, if it existed at all, is likely to have been restricted to the ability to write one's name and probably not much more. An illiterate person, requiring a document to be written or read, would simply have had recourse to a scribe.

Egyptian writings on the subject indicate that literacy was a very desirable acquisition, conferring status, securing a position and providing a means to advancement that might lead ultimately to the very highest office. A thorough training in scribal skills was held to be an essential prerequisite for any young man with professional or political aspirations. There appear to have been elementary schools at which the basic skills were taught; more advanced training was obtained actually in the job, the system being akin to that of 'apprentice' and 'master', the latter in many cases being a father or near-relative.

School texts of the New Kingdom, which form the bulk of our evidence on Egyptian educational methods, indicate that basic reading and writing were laboriously learned by copying out excerpts from well-known 'classics', at first in cursive hieroglyph and then in the hieratic script. Countless such excerpts survive, written in schoolboy hands

34 Limestone ostracon, the largest of its kind, bearing a copy in school-boy hieratic of part of 'The Story of Sinuhe'. Nineteenth Dynasty. H. 88.5 cm. Ashmolean Museum, Oxford.

of varying competence, on scraps of papyrus, wooden tablets or, most commonly, on limestone ostraca. One of the most famous is the Ramesside ostracon, the largest of its 34
kind, which bears a copy of a sizeable portion of a well-known literary text of the Middle Kingdom, 'The Story of Sinuhe'. Like most efforts of this type, it is a poor version of the text. It contains, in the words of the modern editor of the ostracon, 'every kind of mistake – misspellings, confused constructions, and senseless interpolations – which show that its writer did not know, and suggest that he and his instructors did not care, what the words that he was writing meant'. At a higher level pupils progressed to writing texts actually designed for the purpose of training scribes. Such documents are often cast in the form of letters written by one scribe to another and deliberately include strange words, foreign names, technical terms and difficult calculations – all designed to test the pupil thoroughly. A fine example on a papyrus in the British Museum is devoted 35
to one of the favourite themes of such literature: the advantages of the scribal life as compared to alternatives, in this case military conscription. It is executed in a good literary hand, probably that of an advanced student. The three groups written above the main text are thought to be corrections by the instructor of signs that he felt to be not quite properly formed. The passage begins, 'Apply yourself to writing zealously; do not stay your hand . . .', and ends, 'Pleasant and wealth-abounding is your palette and your roll of papyrus'.

35 Advanced exercise in hieratic, including a passage extolling the scribal life. The instructor's corrections are written above. Nineteenth Dynasty. Papyrus Anastasi 5. H. of sheet, approx. 21 cm. BM 10244,4.

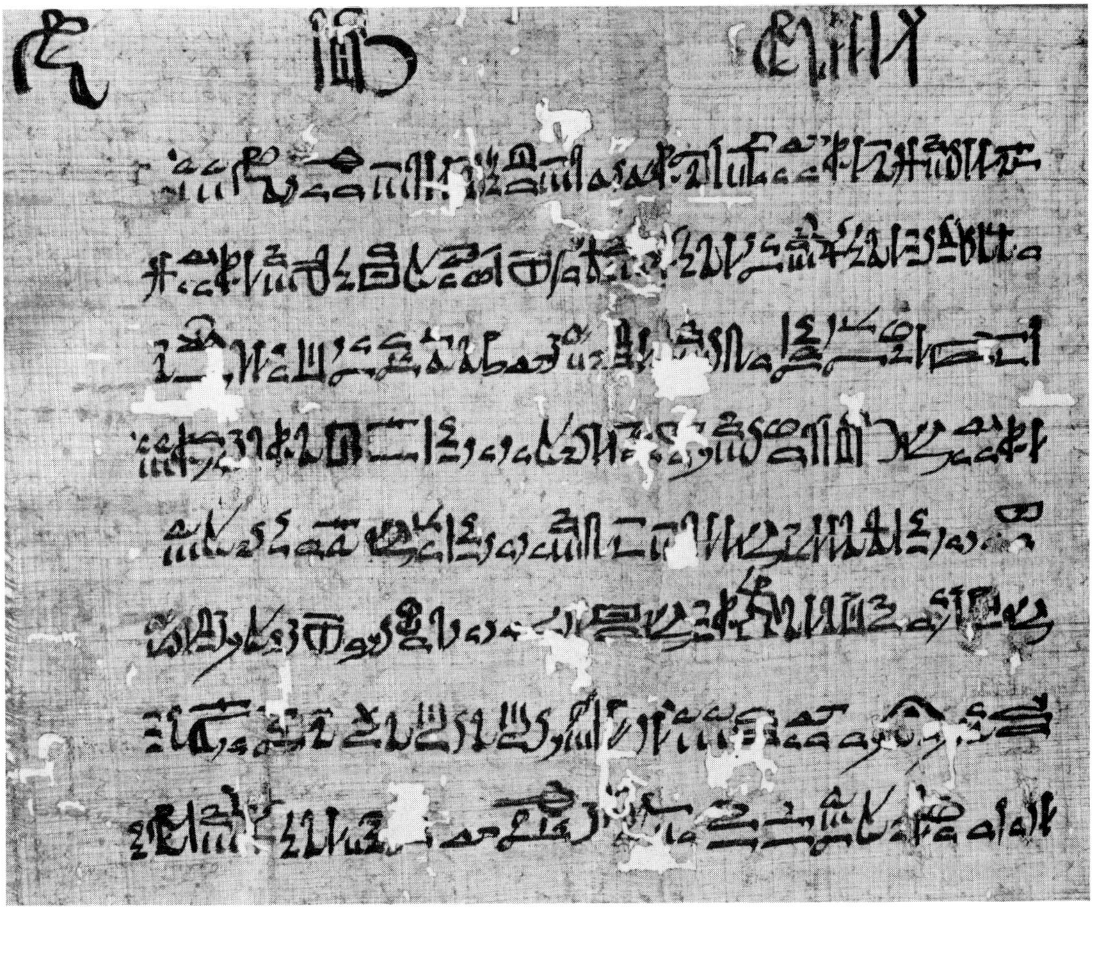

3
The Principles

The Egyptian writing system may be regarded as containing three major types of sign, each of which performs a different function. The first type is the 'logogram', which writes a complete word; the second is the 'phonogram', which represents a sound (a phoneme of the language); the third is the 'determinative', which helps to indicate a word's precise meaning. More broadly, since the logogram and the determinative are both concerned with 'sense' or 'meaning' rather than with 'sound', they can be classed together as 'semograms' (or more traditionally, and less adequately, as 'ideograms'). In the nature of the system there is a certain amount of overlap between the categories, and it is not always easy in practice to distinguish clearly between a semographic and a phonographic usage. Moreover, 'there are degrees and varieties within the groups of sense-signs and sound-signs'. The conventional three-fold division of the system presented here covers the essential ground and provides a useful working model, but it should be kept in mind that the categories are not absolutely hard and fast.

An important feature of the system, seen also in scripts of the Semitic branch, is that it records only the consonantal phonemes; the vowels are not specifically indicated. One of the chief characteristics of both the Egyptian and the Semitic languages is that they contain basic word-roots made up of consonants (usually three in number) that are generally invariable; within these roots such features as grammatical inflexion are often indicated by internal vowel variation. It is thought that the neglect of the vowels in writing is a direct reflection of their 'instability' in relation to the consonants.

By the time of Middle Egyptian there were twenty-four consonants in the language. A complete list is given below under 'uniconsonantal signs'. To render their phonemic values Egyptologists are accustomed to transliterate them, as far as is possible, into modern alphabetic characters, some with additional points or marks written above or below (so-called 'diacritics') to differentiate them.

Logograms

The simplest form of logogram is that in which a word is represented directly by a picture of the object that it actually denotes:

𓇳, depicting the sun, signifies 'sun' (*rʿ*)
𓉐, depicting the ground-plan of a house, signifies 'house' (*pr*)
𓁷, depicting the human face, signifies 'face' (*ḥr*)

A more developed form works through a kind of extension or association of meaning:

𓇳, depicting the sun, signifies 'day' (*rʿ* or *hrw*)
𓏞, depicting writing equipment, signifies 'scribe' or 'writing' (*sẖ*)
𓂻, depicting a pair of legs, signifies 'come' (*ỉw*)

It is clear that a writing system based entirely on such logograms would be quite impractical. Firstly it would require many thousands of signs to cover the vocabulary of a language. Secondly it would find it very difficult to express, clearly and unambiguously, words for things that cannot easily be pictured. It is these considerations, scholars suggest, that, early on, led to the development of the second category of sign, the phonogram.

Phonograms

These were derived by a process of phonetic borrowing, whereby logograms were used to write other words, or parts of words, to which they were unrelated in meaning but with which they happened to share the same consonantal structure. For example:

the logogram 𓂋, *r*, meaning 'mouth', was used as a phonogram with the phonemic value *r*, to write such words as 𓂋, *r*, meaning 'towards' or to represent the phonemic element *r* in a word like 𓂋𓈖, *rn*, 'name'.

the logogram 𓉐, *pr*, meaning 'house', was used as a phonogram with the value *pr*, in words such as 𓉐𓂋𓂻, *pr*, 'go', or 𓉐𓂋𓏏𓇳, *prt*, 'winter'.

the logogram 𓁷, *ḥr*, meaning 'face', was used as a phonogram with the value *ḥr*, in such words as 𓁷𓏤, *ḥr*, 'upon', and 𓁷𓂋𓏏𓇯, *ḥrt*, 'sky'.

The basic principle at work here is that of the *rebus*, whereby 'one thing is shown, but another meant'. By the same principle the English verb 'can' could be written with the picture , representing a (tin) can, or the word 'belief' with the pictures , representing a bee and a leaf. Using this method the Egyptians were able to develop a large corpus of phonographic signs which was more than adequate to meet their linguistic needs. These phonograms fall naturally into three main categories.

1. Uniconsonantal signs, which represent a single consonant; the most important group. There are twenty-six of these including variants:

Sign	Translit.	Sound-value	Sign	Translit.	Sound-value
𓄿	*ꜣ*	glottal stop	𓎛	*ḥ*	emphatic h
𓇋	*ỉ*	i	𓐍	*ḫ*	ch as in Scottish loch
𓇌 𓏭	*y*	y	𓄡	*ẖ*	slightly softer than last
𓂝	*ꜥ*	gutteral, the ayin of the Semitic languages	𓊃 𓋴	*s*	s
𓅱	*w*	w	𓈙	*š*	sh
𓃀	*b*	b	𓈎	*ḳ*	q
𓊪	*p*	p	𓎡	*k*	k
𓆑	*f*	f	𓎼	*g*	hard g
𓅓	*m*	m	𓏏	*t*	t
𓈖	*n*	n	𓍿	*ṯ*	tj
𓂋	*r*	r	𓂧	*d*	d
𓉔	*h*	h	𓆓	*ḏ*	dj

Among these, 𓄿, 𓇋, and 𓅱 are weak consonants. They were readily assimilated in speech to a preceding vowel, especially at the end of a syllable, and consequently were often omitted in writing; the consonant 𓂋 was similarly unstable. Egyptologists sometimes indicate the graphic omission of a consonant by enclosing its transliteration in brackets.

2. Biconsonantal signs, which represent pairs of successive consonants; the largest single group of phonograms, though fewer than a hundred in all. We have already encountered 𓉐, *pr*, and 𓁷, *ḥr*. Here are some others:

Sign	Translit.	Sign	Translit.	Sign	Translit.
	*ꜣw*	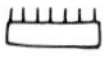	*mn*		*sꜣ*
	*ꜣb* or *mr*		*mr*		*sw*
	*ỉr*		*mr* or *ꜣb*		*sn*
	*wꜣ*		*ms*		*šs*
	*wp*		*nb*		*kꜣ*
	*wr*		*ns*		*tỉ*
	*wḏ*		*ḥm*		*ḏꜣ*
	*bꜣ*		*ḥn*		*ḏd*

3. Triconsonantal signs, which represent groups of three successive consonants. There are between forty and fifty of these, the following being among the most common:

Sign	Transliteration	Sign	Transliteration
	*ỉwn*		*rwḏ*
	*ʿnḫ*	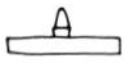	*ḥtp*
	*ʿḥʿ*		*ḫpr*
	*wꜣḥ*		*ḫrw*
	*nfr*		*šmʿ*
	*nṯr*		*tyw*
	*nḏm*		*ḏʿm*

It should be noted that although the signs in the last two categories do occur as individual hieroglyphs, they are more often accompanied by uniconsonantal signs, which record part or even the whole of their phonemic value. This is referred to as 'phonetic complementing'. In general it is a single consonant, more usually the last of the group, that is complemented:

Sign	Translit.	Sign	Translit.	Sign	Translit.
	*3w*		*wr*		*nḏm*
	*w3*		*b3*		*ḫpr*
	*w3ḥ*	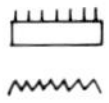	*mn*		

Fuller complementing is, however, by no means rare:

Sign	Translit.	Sign	Translit.	Sign	Translit.
	*b3*		*nfr*	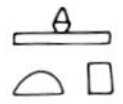	*ḥtp*
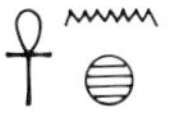	*ʿnḫ*		*ns*	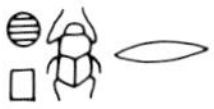	*ḫpr*

The original function of such complements was to emphasise that the complemented sign was indeed a phonogram and not a logogram, but they were also exploited as calligraphic devices, to be deployed, for example, when there was a need to fill an unwanted space.

In theory, the system allowed a word of more than one consonant to be written in a number of different ways. In practice, however, a degree of economy was excercised, with the full range of possibilities being left unexploited and with spellings being relatively standardised. Thus, for example, the preposition *ḥnʿ*, 'together with', is always written  and never as ; the verb *mn*, 'to remain', always takes the form 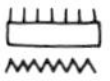 or the like, and is never written as ; the adjective *nfr*, 'good', though written variously as , , or , never lacks the triconsonantal ; and the biconsonantals  and 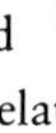, though they can both represent *mr*, are used each in a particular set of words (related by root) and are not interchangeable. Many words do have variant forms but their orthography has a sufficiently consistent 'core' to make them recognisable without undue difficulty. This process of word recognition is further aided by the third major category of sign, the determinative.

Determinatives

Determinatives, which like phonograms were derived from logograms, were placed at the end of words to assist in establishing their meaning, where otherwise there might be uncertainty. For example, a determinative in the form of a stroke was commonly appended to a logogram to emphasise that its function was logographic: , 'sun', , 'face', , 'house'. Similarly, to remove ambiguity, a sign or group of signs subject to more than one interpretation would be written with the determinative appropriate to the intended meaning. Thus the logogram , *sḫ*, would be written , with the determinative depicting a man, when the word 'scribe' was meant, and 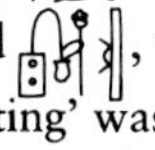, with the determinative representing a book-roll, when the word 'write' or 'writing' was meant. We have already noted in Chapter 2 the use of determinatives (in the form of male and female figures) to disambiguate names. So also with other phonograms. For example, the group 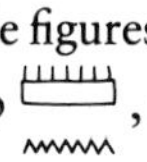, *mn*, could stand for a number of different words, among them 'remain' and

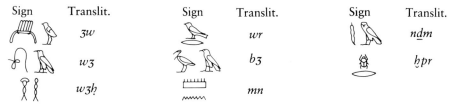

'weak'. To distinguish between them, the former was written 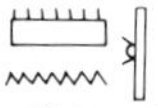, with the book-roll determinative (indicating an abstract notion), the latter , with the determinative of a small bird (indicating something small, bad or weak).

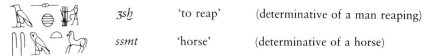

Some determinatives are specific in application, which means that they are closely tied to one word:

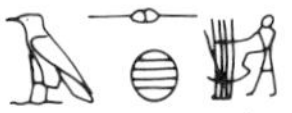	*ꜣsḫ*	'to reap'	(determinative of a man reaping)
	*ssmt*	'horse'	(determinative of a horse)

Others identify a word as belonging to a certain class or category. These are called 'generic determinatives' or 'taxograms'. The following form a small selection:

	man, person		walk, run		metal
	woman		limb, flesh		town, village
	god, king		skin, mammal, leather		desert, foreign country
	force, effort		small, bad, weak		house, building
	eat, drink, speak		wood, tree		book, writing, abstract
	enemy, foreigner		sun, light, time		several, plural
	force, effort		stone		

Words could be written with one determinative or more:

	*ỉkm*	'shield' ('shield' determinative)
	*wšb*	'answer' ('speak' determinative)
	*wgs*	'cut open' ('knife' and 'force' determinatives)
	*bhꜣw*	'fugitives' ('legs', 'man' and 'plural' determinatives)

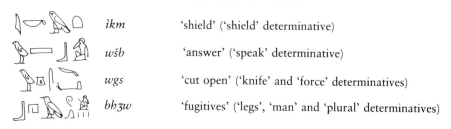

The determinatives of a word could also be changed or varied, so as to indicate a nuance of meaning. Take the word *ỉkm*. It is often followed by the specific determinative as above, but it was also written with the leather or metal determinatives (, ), when it was felt to be important to distinguish its material. The information conveyed by the determinative in either case is additional to that which is implicit in the word *ỉkm* itself. It is a special attribute of the Egyptian system that it could convey by pictorial means extra-linguistic information of this kind.

As well as performing a semantic function, determinatives were useful aids to reading. Since they mark the ends of words, they would have helped the reader to identify the 'word-images' or 'word-pictures' in a continuous text. Such 'images' once established were very slow to change, resulting in a stability for the system which certainly had its advantages but which was also one of the major reasons for the gradual divergence between the written and spoken forms of the language (a divergence already well advanced, it is believed, by the time of the Middle Kingdom). As the one failed to keep pace with the other, the script became increasingly 'historical', with a somewhat fossilised orthography no longer accurately reflecting contemporary pronunciations.

As any routine line of inscription will demonstrate, all the categories of sign mentioned above occur regularly, side by side, in Egyptian writing, sometimes together with other, less important, types, called 'orthograms' and 'calligrams', which convey neither meaning nor sound but may be present for special orthographic or aesthetic reasons:

wḏ ḥm.f ḥr wrryt.f nt ḏꜥm ib.f ꜣw

'His Majesty departed upon his chariot of electrum, his heart joyful'

In this line the signs (*w*), (*f*), (*r*), (*y*), (*n*), (*t*), and (*m*) are uniconsonantal, with (in both cases), , and , acting as phonetic complements; (*wḏ*), (*ḥm*), (*ḥr*), (*wr*), and (*ꜣw*) are biconsonantal; (*ḏꜥm*) is triconsonantal; (*ib* = 'heart') is a logogram; the first is an orthogram; and , , , , and are determinatives.

Such apparent complexity has led the Egyptian system (and others like it) to be treated rather disparagingly by many commentators. Dismissing it as 'cumbrous' and 'illogical', they have found it difficult to understand 'the process of thought by which it was evolved, and even more difficult to imagine why it should have continued with so little development over so long a period'. The central complaint is that the Egyptians, evidently lacking in imagination, failed to take what is deemed to be the 'obvious step': simply to use their uniconsonantal signs in the manner of an alphabet, abandoning the other types of sign. Such criticism, which is based essentially on the assumed superiority of alphabetic scripts over all others, is quite misplaced. It not only overrates the efficiency of alphabetic systems, it also seriously undervalues the merits of others. The Egyptian system has the 'disadvantage' of containing a relatively large number of signs. In compensation, however, its mixed orthography creates visually distinctive word patterns that actually enhance legibility. Direct support for this view is provided by those few attempts at 'alphabetic' writing, which were carried out, perhaps experimentally under the influence of Greek, during Egypt's Late Period. The experiment, if such it was, was short-lived and it is not hard to see why. These 'alphabetic' texts, consisting of a succession of consonantal signs, written in unbroken sequence like Greek of the time, are very difficult to read, considerably more so than contemporary inscriptions written in the traditional orthography. The verdict of one percipient authority is that 'writing Egyptian with only an alphabet of consonants sacrificed legibility to simplicity, and thus did more harm than good . . . Perhaps it is now time to stop chiding the Egyptians for not "taking the step which seems to us so obvious"'.

There is, of course, a further dimension to the matter. The reduction of the system in the way suggested would have meant the abandonment of what was evidently to the Egyptians an exceedingly important attribute of the script: namely, its capacity, because of its pictorial and unrestricted nature, to be exploited for purposes other than straightforward linguistic communication. Some of the ways in which the hieroglyphs functioned as part of a larger system of artistic representation were mentioned in the previous chapter, where certain non-scriptorial uses and significances were also noted, while earlier in this chapter attention was drawn to the script's ability to convey 'extra-linguistic' information. It is relevant to add here the way in which the script could be manipulated to produce so-called 'sportive' or 'cryptographic' writings, designed, it has been suggested, 'to clothe a religious text in mystery' or simply 'to intrigue the reader'. The extent to which such manipulation was possible is shown most strikingly by the systems of orthography employed in certain temple inscriptions of the Ptolemaic and Roman Periods. They are characterised, among other things, by an enormous increase in the number of signs and variants, in the values and meanings that the signs could bear, and in the possible combinations of signs and sign-groups, an elaboration achieved not by artificial means but simply by exploiting to the full the inherent properties of the hieroglyphic script. To a reader accustomed only to the classical orthography these texts are unintelligible, though it is now doubted that they were actually designed to be deliberately cryptographic. Whatever the reason for such elaboration, it is clear that it was not an original invention of the Ptolemaic Period. On the contrary, it was the final stage of a tradition that is strongly in evidence already in the New Kingdom and can be traced back sporadically as far as the Old Kingdom. Indeed some 'sportive' writings are to be found as regular components of the standard system from a relatively early date. A prime example is the common occurrence, from the Middle Kingdom on, of the hieroglyph , as an abbreviated writing of the title  *ỉmy-r*, 'overseer'. The basis of the usage, which is a 'kind of graphic pun', becomes clear, when it is understood that  represents a tongue and that the title *ỉmy-r* means literally 'he who is in the mouth'.

Vocalisation

The general absence of vowel notation means that our modern transliterations represent only the consonantal skeletons of Egyptian words. Many of these are difficult to communicate verbally, being, as they stand, virtually unpronouncable. As an aid, therefore, to pronunciation (in discussion, lectures, teaching), Egyptologists insert a short 'e' between the consonants and render ꜣ and ʿ as 'a'. Thus, for example:

sꜣ	'sa'	*ḥnʿ*	'hena'
wrs	'weres'	*ʿḏʿ*	'adja'
mn	'men'	*nfrt*	'nefret'
wbn	'weben'	*sḥtp*	'sehetep'

It must always be borne in mind, however, that the resulting vocalisations are artificial devices serving as a convenience and bear little or no relation to the ancient pronunciation of the words.

Our knowledge of the original pronunciation of Egyptian is very incomplete but not a total blank. The vocalic structure of a considerable number of words can be deduced from their form in Coptic, the last stage of Egyptian and the only stage in which the vowels are written. Although Coptic contains a large number of Greek and other foreign words, the bulk of its vocabulary is of Pharaonic ancestry, in many cases going back to the earliest stages of the language. A selection is given below of some common Egyptian words together with their Coptic descendants:

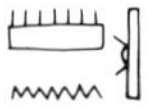	*mn* (remain)	ⲙⲟⲩⲛ	(moun)
	*mdw* (speak)	ⲙⲟⲩⲧⲉ	(moute)
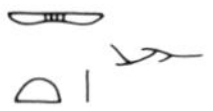	*pḏt* (bow)	ⲡⲓⲧⲉ	(pite)
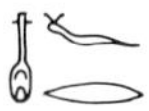	*nfr* (good)	ⲛⲟⲩϥⲉ	(nūfe)
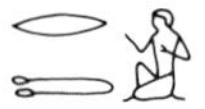	*r(m)ṯ* (man)	ⲣⲱⲙⲉ	(rōme)

	*rꜥ* (sun)	ⲣⲏ	(rē)
	*sf* (yesterday)	ⲥⲁϥ	(saf)
	*kmt* (Egypt)	ⲕⲏⲙⲉ	(kēme)

The Coptic forms cannot, of course, be accepted as accurate indications of the way in which the words were actually pronounced in earlier periods. Coptic is the end product of centuries, even millennia, of linguistic evolution, in the course of which the grammar of Egyptian, including its phonology, was subject to constant modification and change. One has only to consider that Coptic is separated from Old Egyptian by over 2,000 years – a span of time that is twice as long as that which covers the evolution of modern English from Anglo-Saxon – to realise the potential for change. Coptic is the single most important source of information on the Egyptian vocalic system but its evidence must be used with caution.

There are other, earlier sources of evidence on the subject. A number of ancient scripts (for example, Greek, Assyrian, Babylonian), which themselves indicate vowels, contain fully vocalised transcriptions of contemporary Egyptian words. Such evidence is invaluable, though unfortunately it is very limited in quantity and scope. The earliest and most important of these transcriptions occur in cuneiform documents contemporary with the New Kingdom in Egypt. They include the names of several Egyptian kings, among them such well known ones as *'Imn-ḥtp* (Amenophis) and *Rꜥ-mss* (Ramesses), which are transcribed as *Amanhatpi* and *Riamesesa* respectively.

Such vocalisations coupled with careful inferences from the Coptic evidence have enabled scholars to make considerable headway in ascertaining the rules governing Egyptian syllabic structure and vowel quantity and even to get some idea of the quality of the vowels. The indications are that up to the Eighteenth Dynasty Egyptian had only three vowels, namely 'a', 'i' and 'u', all of which could be either long or short. The vowels 'e' and 'o' were relatively late developments.

It should be mentioned at this point that some scholars disagree with the conventional view, followed above, that the phonograms are essentially consonantal. They argue that these signs are really syllabic, standing, in the case of the 'uniconsonantal' signs, for consonant + any vowel. The question is too complex to consider in detail here. Suffice it to say that the 'syllabic' interpretation fits very well with current theories on script development, but is problematic in other respects and is generally rejected by Egyptologists. This theory should not, incidentally, be confused with the phenomenon referred to in Egyptological literature as 'syllabic orthography', also called 'group writing'. This is a method of writing characterised, among other things, by the use of biconsonantal signs, or pairs of uniconsonantal signs, instead of single uniconsonantal signs (for example, 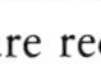, *ꜥꜣ*, for *ꜥ*; 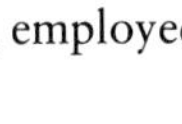, *hꜣ*, for *h*). In such groups the second element is often a weak consonant indicating the presence of a vowel. Employed mostly to write words of foreign origin, this kind of orthography was particularly popular during the New Kingdom, when its wider usage may have been encouraged by the example of the contemporary cuneiform system, employed very generally throughout Western Asia, in which the vowels are recorded.

Origins

Although the principles underlying Egyptian writing are now fairly well understood, it is still unclear how the system came into being in the first place. Was it the end-product of a process of gradual development or was it the invention of a single person? Was it indigenous or was it introduced from abroad? It is impossible to give definitive answers to these questions. All that can be said in the present state of knowledge is that some alternatives seem more probable than others. Unfortunately, the Egyptians themselves give us no direct help on the subject of the origin of their script. Hieroglyphic writing was traditionally regarded by them as the invention of the gods, in particular of Thoth, the divine scribe, who is often referred to in texts as the 'lord of writing'. We are left to deduce what we can, therefore, from the evidence provided by the earliest examples of the script itself.

Writing makes its first appearance in Egypt at the very end of the Predynastic Period, in the reigns of the immediate predecessors of the kings of the First Dynasty. That it should do so at this time is not altogether surprising. It was a period of great cultural change and technological innovation, with a system of government increasingly concentrated around the royal court. It is reasonable to see writing, within this context, as itself a new technology, invented, or adopted, in response to the needs of the system; the ways in which it was used suggest that it served to further central control both ideologically and administratively.

To the ideological category belong those inscriptions that occur on a series of votive objects decorated with representations in low relief – the first examples of Egyptian
36 a,b 'monumental' art. The most famous of these objects is the palette of King Narmer, in which the king is represented engaged in acts symbolic of his status and authority. The administrative function is to be seen in those labels or dockets usually written in ink, or
37 roughly incised, on the outsides of stone and pottery vessels. The inscriptions in both contexts are short and restricted. They consist almost wholly of titles and names (personal, mainly royal, names, place-names and the names of commodities). In the case of the vessels they identify the owner, the contents and sometimes the source. In the case of the ornamental objects, where the hieroglyphs form an integral part of a larger scene, they identify the representations with which they are associated – the unity between 'caption' and 'figure' in these latter, carefully carved cases, showing clearly how in style and form the hieroglyphs were direct offshoots of the new pictorial art of the period.

Few of these early inscriptions are completely unambiguous. It is not simply a matter of unfamiliar vocabulary. The signary itself had yet to stabilise into its standard dynastic form. It contains several hieroglyphs that do not survive into later usage and whose reading, therefore, can only be guessed at. What is clear, however, is that the basic 'mixed' structure of the writing system is already fully formed – it consists not only of logograms but of phonograms as well; moreover, all the different types of phonogram (uni- and multi-consonantal signs) are present. Thus, for example, among the signs that
37 can be definitely identified on the pottery vessel, the Horus-bird, 𓅃, denoting the king as 'the Horus' is a logogram, while 𓇓, 𓇋, and 𓊪 are phonograms, the last two unicon-
36 sonantal (*ỉ* and *p*), the first triconsonantal (*šmꜥ*). In the case of the palette, in addition to what is traditionally regarded as a *rebus* writing the king's name, Narmer (the two hieroglyphs, 𓆡 , and 𓌻, one depicting a cat-fish, the other a chisel, supplying the phonetic values *nꜥr* and *mr* respectively), there are, among others, the phonograms 𓂝, *wꜥ* and 𓈙, *š*, quite possibly writing a name *wꜥš* and 𓍿, *ṯ*, and 𓏏, *t*, combined in what is probably an abbreviated writing of the title *ṯꜣty*, 'vizier'. In short, although it was to be some considerable time before its potential was fully exploited – long continuous texts, for example, are not known before the early Old Kingdom – the writing system, already at its inception or very shortly afterwards, had the capacity to express almost everything that was later to be required of it. Elsewhere in the Near East writing is first

36(a) *Left* Slate palette of King Narmer, obverse. The King is represented as the dominant figure smiting an enemy with a mace, in a pose that was to become part of standard royal iconography. His name, written above him with two hieroglyphs, one depicting a cat-fish, the other a chisel, is enclosed in a rectangular structure called the *serekh*. The other figures in the scene are also labelled. Hierakonpolis. Late Predynastic Period. H. 63 cm. Cairo Museum, JE 32169.

36(b) *Below left* Slate palette of King Narmer, reverse. The King is shown in the upper register engaged in a ritual procession. His name occurs twice, written with the same signs as on the obverse, once in a *serekh*, once without. Other identifiable hieroglyphs are present.

37 *Above* Pottery vessel with ink label in cursive hieroglyphs, now somewhat faded. The intelligible signs include a *serekh* enclosing a king's name possibly to be read as *Ka*, surmounted by a falcon denoting the royal title 'Horus'. To the right are three hieroglyphs, *šmʿ*, *ỉ* and *p*, which can be read as *ỉp-šmʿ*, 'tax of Upper Egypt' or the like. Abydos. Late Predynastic Period. H. 27 cm. BM 35508.

attested in contexts of record-keeping and accounting, and the indications seem to be that it developed gradually out of a system of numerical notation. No such 'prehistory' is convincingly traceable for Egyptian writing. On present evidence, admittedly sparse and possibly very misleading, it appears to come into use almost 'ready-made', as it were.

It is generally thought unlikely that full writing could have been invented independently in more than one place in the ancient Near East. This belief coupled with the apparently sudden appearance of writing in a developed form in Egypt has led to the suggestion that the Egyptian system was borrowed from outside. The areas of Mesopotamia and Elam have been cited as the most likely sources, where in the last quarter or so of the fourth millennium BC a pictographic system, similar in appearance and structure to the hieroglyphic script, was used to write first the Sumerian language and then, a little later, the language known as Proto-Elamite. On present estimates the earliest Sumerian writing appears to ante-date the first hieroglyphs by a century or more. That there was contact between Egypt and these areas is beyond doubt. Mesopotamian and Elamite influences are discernible in a number of features of Egyptian culture during the late Predynastic Period, most clearly in the form of various artistic designs and motifs (the intertwined felines on the reverse of Narmer's palette are a case in point). The importation of writing into Egypt can, therefore, be viewed, it has been suggested, as part of a larger process of cultural transmission.

Reasonable as this hypothesis is, there can be no question of the Egyptian system being a direct borrowing of the Sumerian. One obvious objection is that there is little, if any, discernible overlap between the two sets of signs. The Egyptian signary, though pictographic in character like archaic Sumerian, is clearly derived from indigenous sources. Several of the hieroglyphs depict objects, such as certain kinds of tool and weapon, that are known from the archaeological record to have been in contemporary use in Egypt. Others have representational antecedents among the motifs and designs on painted pottery of the earlier Predynastic Period and among the 'mnemonic' symbols, thought to mark possession or ownership, that occur on pots and implements of the same date. More importantly, although both are mixed systems, their structures are not the same. In the first place, the balance of their 'mix' is different. In the earliest Sumerian logography is predominant. Phonography is present at first to a very limited extent, and takes several centuries to become fully developed. By comparison the earliest Egyptian, as noted above, is a system that already contains a substantial, if not complete, phonographic component, in this respect being considerably more advanced than the contemporary Sumerian. In the second place the basic phonetic unit of the system is different in each case. Sumerian is syllabic; its signs represent syllables of the language, each one consisting either of a vowel or of a consonant plus a vowel. Egyptian, on the other hand, is consonantal; its signs represent only the consonants of the language; the vowels, being 'unstable', are not specifically recorded. These differences are rooted in the structures of the languages that the two scripts represent. They are so fundamental as to be decisive against the theory that one system was simply borrowed from the other. The present consensus is, therefore, that if Egyptian writing is to be regarded as not wholly indigenous and Sumerian is to be seen as somehow influential in its invention, then the influence was imparted through a process of what has been called 'stimulus diffusion'; in other words, Sumerian provided the example or the idea of writing, together with some of its operating principles, not the system itself.

4
A Little Basic Grammar

Egyptian grammar is a large and complicated subject, important areas of which are still imperfectly understood. It cannot, without distortion, be reduced to a series of simple rules. This present chapter is intended merely to give a flavour – to a non-Egyptological readership – of how the language works. It is *highly selective* and is confined to Middle Egyptian, the 'classical' stage of the language and the one with which the study of Egyptian is usually begun. It includes also a brief account of other important topics; numerals, kings' names, dates and the offering formula.

Gender and number

There are two genders in Egyptian, masculine and feminine. Masculine nouns have no special ending; feminine nouns end in 𓏏, *t*.

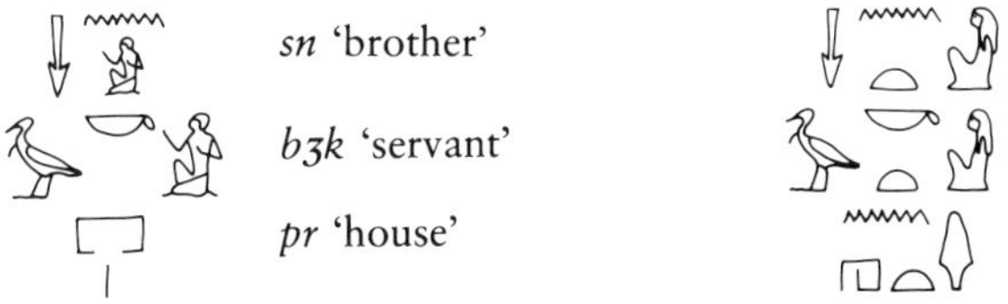

sn 'brother' — *snt* 'sister'

bꜣk 'servant' — *bꜣkt* '(female) servant'

pr 'house' — *nht* 'tree'

There are three numbers, singular, plural and dual. The plural endings are 𓅱, *w*, for masculine and 𓅱𓏏, *wt*, for feminine, though the 𓅱 is often omitted in writing. The determinative of plurality, written 𓏥 or 𓏪 is normally present at the end of plural words.

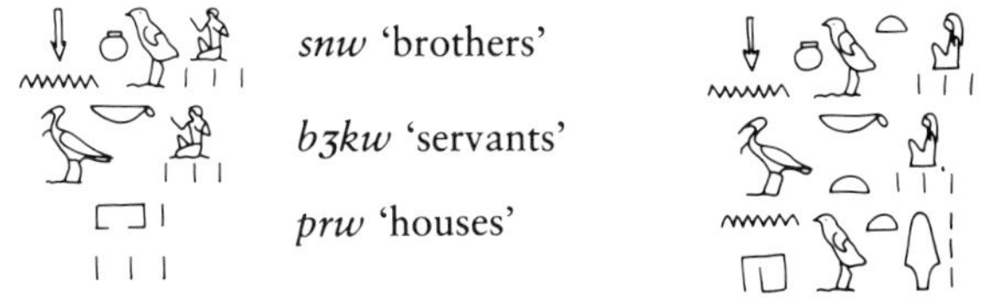

snw 'brothers' — *snwt* 'sisters'

bꜣkw 'servants' — *bꜣkwt* '(female) servants'

prw 'houses' — *nhwt* 'trees'

The dual is used for pairs of things. The masculine ending is 𓅱𓏭, *wy*, the feminine is 𓏏𓏭, *ty*:

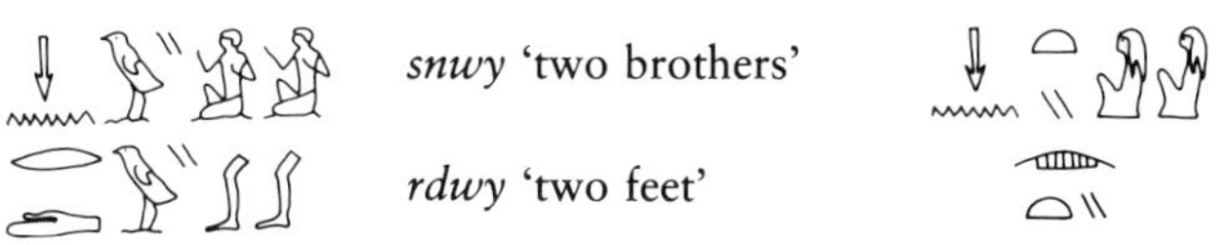

snwy 'two brothers' — *snty* 'two sisters'

rdwy 'two feet' — *spty* 'two lips'

Adjectives take their gender and number from the noun they describe and are placed after the noun:

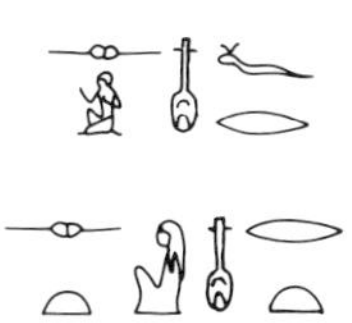

s nfr 'good man'

st nfrt 'good woman'

	*pr ꜥꜣ*	'big house'
	*nht ꜥꜣt*	'big tree'
	*snw ỉḳrw*	'excellent brothers'
	*snwt ỉḳrwt*	'excellent sisters'

The article and co-ordination

There are no direct equivalents of the English definite and indefinite articles, 'the' and 'a'. Thus, for example, , *pr*, may be rendered 'house', 'a house' or 'the house' according to context. Similarly there is no special word for 'and', co-ordination being expressed more often than not by direct juxtapositioning:

 *sn snt* 'brother and sister'

 *nṯrw nṯrwt* 'gods and goddesses'

The cases

Egyptian is not an inflected language, like Latin or German. There are no case-endings to indicate the syntactic function of a noun. Whether a noun is the subject or the object of a verb is indicated by its position in a sentence, the normal word order being verb + noun-subject + noun-object:

 (verb)  (subject)  (object)

sḏm s ḫrw, 'the man hears the voice'

The genitive is expressed in two ways, direct and indirect. In the direct genitive the second noun follows the first without a connecting link. It is thought that in this form the genitive expresses a particularly close relationship:

 *nbt pr* 'mistress of the house'  *sꜣ Rꜥ* 'son of Re'

In the indirect genitive the second noun is preceded by the genitival adjective , *n(y)*, plural , *nw*, which agrees in number and gender with the first noun:

	*sbꜣ n pr*	'door of the house'
	*nỉwt nt nḥḥ*	'city of eternity'
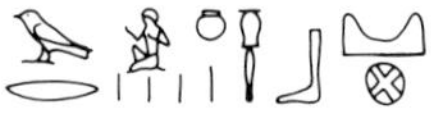	*wrw nw ꜣbḏw*	'great ones of Abydos'

When the genitive is pronominal it is expressed by the so-called suffix pronoun, the forms and meanings of which are as follows:

	*ỉ*	'my'	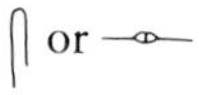	*s*	'her', 'its'
	*k*	'your' (masculine singular)		*n*	'our'
	*ṯ*	'your' (feminine singular)	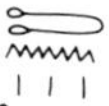	*ṯn*	'your' (plural)
	*f*	'his'	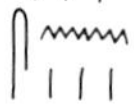	*sn*	'their'

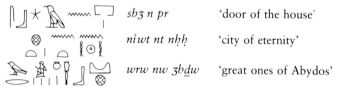

 *pr.ỉ* 'my house'  *sn.k* 'your brother'

 *nỉwt.n* 'our town'  *b3kw.sn* 'their servants'

These pronouns serve also as the subject of verbs and the object of prepositions (see below). Note that in transliteration it is customary to place a dot before a suffix.

The dative is rendered simply by means of the preposition  , *n*, 'to' or 'for', which always precedes its object, whether noun or pronoun:

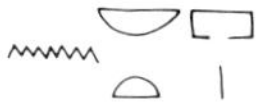 *n nbt pr* 'for the mistress of the house'  *n.s* 'for her'

Prepositions

The most common prepositions are:

 *m* 'in, from, with'

 n 'to, for'

 *r* 'to, towards'

 *ḫr* 'before, under'

 *ḥr* 'upon'

 *ẖr* 'under'

 *m pr* 'in the house'

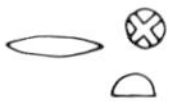 *r nỉwt* 'towards the town'

 *ẖr rdwy* 'under the feet'

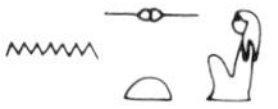 *n st* 'for the woman'

 *ḥr t3* 'upon the land'

 *ḫr nswt* 'before the King'

Such phrases are usually placed at the end or towards the end of a clause:

sḏm s ḫrw m pr

'the man hears the voice in the house'

Sentences

Sentence structure and, in particular, the nature and role of the verb, are the most problematic areas of Egyptian grammar. The traditional view is that there are two types of sentence in Egyptian, verbal and non-verbal. Although according to present theory this is not an accurate formulation, it may still serve for the practical purpose of translating Egyptian into English. It is important to note that, in Egyptian, distinctions of 'tense' and 'mood' and the difference between 'main' and 'subordinate' clauses are rarely indicated clearly in the writing and can often only be determined by reference to the context.

In the non-verbal sentence the link between subject and predicate is left unexpressed:

 *rʿ m pt* 'the sun (is, was) in the sky'

 *nb m pr* 'the master (is, was) in the house'

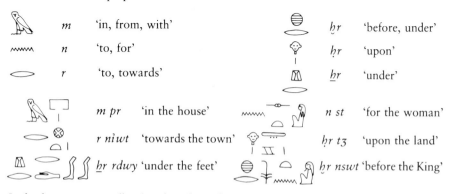

In the verbal sentence the predicate is a verb, most typically one belonging to the so-called 'suffix-conjugation', the basic pattern of which is verb stem + suffix-pronoun.

Egyptologists refer to it as the *sḏm.f* (sedjemef) form, after the verb traditionally used as the model. The *sḏm.f* is not a simple unity. Owing to the lack of vowel notation, the word as written 'conceals' several different forms, each of which has its own meaning. The most frequently encountered is the 'indicative' *sḏm.f*, which expresses an event as an objective fact. Conventionally translated as a present tense, it is actually 'tenseless', and, depending on context, may have past and future, as well as present, reference. It conjugates as follows:

sḏm.ỉ	'I hear'	*sḏm.s*	'she, it, hears'
sḏm.k	'you (masc.) hear'	*sḏm.n*	'we hear'
sḏm.ṯ	'you (fem.) hear'	*sḏm.ṯn*	'you hear'
sḏm.f	'he hears'	*sḏm.sn*	'they hear'

The subject of the verb may also, of course, be a noun, which, like the pronoun, follows the verb, as in the sentence 'the man hears the voice' cited above.

The numerals

The numerals are denoted by seven special signs:

wꜥ	1	*ḏbꜥ*	10,000
mḏw	10	*ḥfnw*	100,000
št	100		
ḫ3	1,000	*ḥḥ*	1,000,000

When written together to form a single number they are placed in descending order of magnitude. Multiples of each are indicated by simple repetition of the sign:

7 =   369 =

24 =   142,235 =

The numeral is placed after the noun, which is generally in the singular:

s 7 'seven men'   *nỉwt ḫ3* 'a thousand towns'

The King's names

When a king ascended the throne he assumed five 'great names', the two principal among them being what Egyptologists call the *prenomen* and the *nomen*. These names are easily distinguished because they are enclosed within so-called 'cartouches' or royal rings: . The Egyptian name for the cartouche was , *šnw* (shenu), 'that which encircles'. It is thought that the cartouche symbolised the fact that the bearer of the name ruled over everything that the sun encircles. The *prenomen* is often preceded by the titles , *nṯr nfr*, 'good god', , *nb t3wy*, 'lord of the two lands', and, most importantly, , *nswt-bỉty*, 'King of Upper and Lower Egypt', while the *nomen* is introduced by , *s3 Rꜥ*, 'son of Re'. Frequently the epithet , *dỉ ꜥnḫ*, 'given life', or, *dỉ ꜥnḫ ḏt*, 'given life eternally', follows the names. Here is a titulary featuring the names of Tuthmosis III of the Eighteenth Dynasty:

nṯr nfr nb tꜣwy nswt-bỉty Mn-ḫpr-Rꜥ sꜣ Rꜥ Ḏḥwty-ms dỉ ꜥnḫ ḏt

'The good god, lord of the two lands, king of Upper and Lower Egypt, Men-kheper-Re, son of Re, Tuthmosis, given life eternally'

The ordinary word for king, already encountered above, is *nswt*, often abbreviated to. Here are some other common designations with their conventional translations:

	ḥm	'majesty'
	ỉty	'sovereign'
	nb	'lord'
	pr-ꜥꜣ	'great house' (= 'Pharaoh', used from the New Kingdom on)

Such designations are often followed by the 'wish formula', *ꜥnḫ(w) wḏꜣ(w) snb(w)*, 'may he live, be prosperous, be healthy', usually abbreviated to .

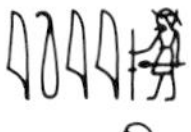

Dates

Dating in Egypt was not continual but was based on the year of the reigning king. The year was subdivided into seasons, months and days. The full system consists of the following categories:

1. regnal year		*ḥꜣt-sp*	
2. month (four in a season)		*tpy*	(the first month)
		ꜣbd	(the remaining months)
3. season (three in a year)		*ꜣḫt*	(inundation)
		prt	(winter)
		šmw	(summer)
4. day (thirty in a month)		*sw*	

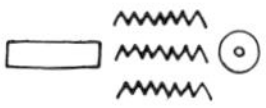

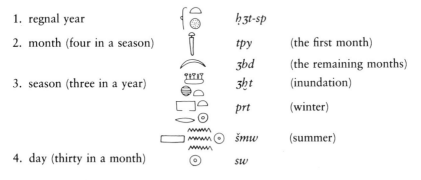

Here are some typical dates:

ḥꜣt-sp 2 ꜣbd 3 ꜣḫt sw 1
'year 2, month 3 of the inundation season, day 1' (of the reigning king)

ḥꜣt-sp 12 tpy prt sw 11
'year 12, month 1 of winter, day 11' (of the reigning king)

Commonly, dates are abbreviated giving only the year of the king, as on a stela in the British Museum: 38

38 Hieroglyphic inscription from a stela mentioning year nineteen of King Nubkaure (Ammenemes II). Twelfth Dynasty. BM 583.

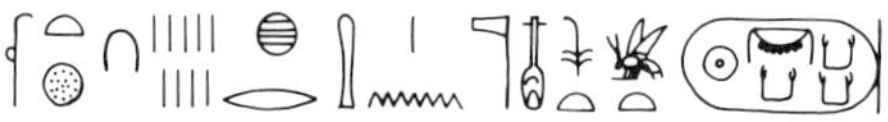

ḥ3t-sp 19 *ḫr ḥm n nṯr nfr nswt-bỉty Nbw-k3w-rʿ*

'year 19 under the majesty of the good god, king of Upper and Lower Egypt, Nub-kau-re' (Ammenemes II of the Twelfth Dynasty)

The offering formula

A very large number of Egyptian texts, particularly those on funerary stelae, begin with the hieroglyphs, *ḥtp dỉ nswt*, probably to be translated as 'an offering which the king gives' or similar. It is referred to by Egyptologists as the 'offering formula' or the 'hetep-di-neswt-formula'. A common variant of the formula, *ḥtp dỉ ʾInpw*, 'an offering which Anubis gives', has already been encountered on the panel of Iry. Its purpose was to procure for a named beneficiary a perpetual supply of the provisions deemed necessary for continued existence in the after-life. The underlying idea seems to have been that the king first provided for the gods, prominent among them, *Wsỉr*, 'Osiris', and, *ʾInpw*, 'Anubis', and that they in turn provided for the dead person or, more strictly, for the dead person's, *k3*, 'spirit'. In the full writing of the formula, the provisions invoked from the gods are collectively referred to as, *prt-ḫrw*, conventionally rendered as 'invocation offerings' and are then individually itemised. The standard provisions are:, *t*, 'bread',, *ḥnkt*, 'beer',, *k3w*, 'oxen',, *3pdw*, 'fowl',, *šs*, 'alabaster', and, *mnḫt*, 'clothing'. The following is a typical example:

ḥtp dỉ nswt Wsỉr nb Ḏdw nb 3bḏw dỉ.f prt-ḫrw t ḥnkt k3w 3pdw šs mnḫt n k3 n nbt pr Mrrt

'an offering which the king gives (to) Osiris, lord of Busiris, lord of Abydos, that he may give invocation offerings (consisting of) bread, beer, oxen, fowl, alabaster and clothing, for the spirit of the mistress of the house, Mereret'

5
Decipherment

The spread of Christianity in Egypt, and the consequent development of the Coptic script, sounded the final death-knell for the ancient 'pagan' writing system. The evidence suggests that by the end of the fifth century AD knowledge of how to read and write the old scripts was extinct. A long dark age – destined to last thirteen centuries and more – descended upon the ancient records. The break in knowledge was complete. The hieroglyphs were fully surrendered to the larger myth of ancient Egypt – the land of strange customs and esoteric wisdom – fostered and handed down by classical writers. Although the Egyptians had been respected throughout classical antiquity as the inventors of writing, this respect does not seem to have been attended by any serious attempt to understand the basic principles of their writing system. The belief that the hieroglyphs, as opposed to the everyday 'popular' script, were not elements of an ordinary writing system but were somehow symbolic and imbued with secret meaning had already become well rooted by the time the historian Diodorus Siculus visited Egypt in the century before Christ: 'their writing does not express the intended concept by means of syllables joined to one another, but by means of the significance of the objects which have been copied, and by its figurative meaning which has been impressed upon the memory by practice.' During the early centuries AD, this 'figurative meaning' received further elaboration. For the influential philosopher Plotinus, writing in the third century, the hieroglyphs were nothing less than Platonic ideas in visual form, 'each picture ... a kind of understanding and wisdom', revealing to the initiated true knowledge as to the essence and substance of things.

Within, and out of, this tradition, there grew a genre of literature specially devoted to the explanation of hieroglyphs. The best preserved and most famous treatise on the subject is the *Hieroglyphika* of Horapollo, which was probably compiled in the fourth or fifth century AD. Here is one of its entries:

> 'What they mean by a vulture
> When they mean a mother, a sight, or boundaries, or foreknowledge ... they draw a vulture. A mother, since there is no male in this species of animal ... the vulture stands for sight since of all other animals the vulture has the keenest vision.... It means boundaries, because when a war is about to break out, it limits the place in which the battle will occur, hovering over it for seven days. Foreknowledge, because of what has been said above and because it looks forward to the amount of corpses which the slaughter will provide it for food ...'

There is a germ of truth in this account, in as much as the Egyptian word for 'mother', , *mwt*, is written with the hieroglyph representing a vulture, but the 'explanations', conceived wholly in allegorical terms, are otherwise complete fantasy.

The importance of the *Hieroglyphika*, however, lies not in its content but in the influence that it exerted over the formation and direction of later opinion and research. When, following the Renaissance in Europe, there arose a new curiosity in things Egyptian, the Neoplatonic tradition, embodied in such 'authoritative' ancient sources as Horapollo, encouraged a line of research that was to prove a long blind alley for scholars attempting to elucidate the 'enigmatic' hieroglyphs. A good example of its influence is to be seen in the conclusions reached after years of extensive study by the German polymath Athanasius Kircher (1602–80). A linguist of great ability, Kircher's translations of hieroglyphic texts, based entirely on preconceived notions as to their symbolic functioning, are wholly wide of the mark, to the point of absurdity. One oft-quoted example may suffice. The name of the king Apries written in hieroglyphs was taken by Kircher to mean 'the benefits of the divine Osiris are to be procured by means of sacred ceremonies and of the chain of the Genii, in order that the benefits of the Nile may be obtained'. Despite his mistaken views of the meaning of the hieroglyphs, Kircher, nevertheless, occupies an honourable place in Egyptological history. He was the author of the first Coptic grammar and vocabulary, works that proved to be an enormous stimulus to the development of Coptic studies. Since knowledge of Coptic was to be a vital element in the eventual decipherment of the hieroglyphs, modern Egyptology owes a considerable debt to the pioneering efforts of Kircher in this field.

Though the myth of the secret hieroglyphs was to remain deeply entrenched, the century following Kircher's death saw a generally more cautious approach to their interpretation. While Kircher's translations were wholly rejected, few complete solutions were offered as alternatives. In 1785 the French orientalist C. J. de Guignes (1721–1800), tried to prove the unity of the Egyptian and Chinese scripts, under the false belief that China had been an Egyptian colony. More valuable, and to the point, was his elaboration of an idea first mooted in 1762 by another French scholar, J. J. Barthélemy (1716–95), that the rings or 'cartouches' to be observed frequently in Egyptian texts enclosed royal names. This was the first hint of a breakthrough, but in the state of knowledge then prevailing the means of making further progress were lacking. In due course, following the discovery of the Rosetta Stone, the means became available and the royal cartouche was to prove the very key that unlocked the secrets of the hieroglyphs.

39 The Rosetta Stone was discovered in July, 1799, near the town of Rashid, ancient Rosetta, which is situated in the Delta, on the western arm of the Nile near the sea. It was unearthed, quite fortuitously, by a gang of French soldiers who were part of Napoleon Bonaparte's invading army. Under the command of an officer named Pierre Bouchard, they were digging foundations for a fort and, according to one account, found the monument built into an ancient wall. The 'stone' – a substantial slab of black basalt, 118 cm high, 77 cm wide, 30 cm thick, and weighing 762 kg – is actually a commemorative stela, which was once set up in an Egyptian temple. It is broken and was probably about 50 cm or so higher when intact. Incised on one face, it bears an inscription dated to year 9 of the reign of Ptolemy V Epiphanes, corresponding to 27 March 196 BC, the main part of which is a copy of a decree issued by a general council of Egyptian priests recording the honours bestowed upon the king by the temples of Egypt. The point of crucial importance about the inscription is that it is reproduced in three different scripts: hieroglyphic at the top, demotic in the middle, and Greek at the bottom. None of the sections has escaped damage, the worst affected being the hieroglyphic. The bilingual nature of the text and the potential that this offered, since Greek was a known language, for the decipherment of the Egyptian versions, were immediately apparent to the French *savants* who first examined the stone after its transference to Cairo. To their enormous credit they lost no time in making ink impressions of the inscriptions and in distributing them among the scholars of Europe. After the defeat of Napoleon's army, the stone itself, which had been moved to Alexandria, was ceded to the British in 1801, together with other antiquities, under Article XVI of the Treaty of Alexandria. It was shipped back to Britain in February, 1802, and was deposited for some months at the Society of Antiquaries of London, where a translation of the Greek section was read out in April of that year by the Rev. Stephen Weston and where further reproductions were subsequently made. It was transferred to the British Museum towards the end of 1802, where it remains to the present day.

39 The Rosetta Stone bearing a single text written in three different scripts: hieroglyphic at the top, demotic in the middle, Greek at the bottom. 196 BC. H. 1.18 m. BM 24.

The distribution of the various copies of the stone inaugurated a period of intense study, with scholars competing anxiously and even jealously to be the first to achieve the prize of decipherment. The 'devil of hieroglyphics', as it has been called, was let loose in no uncertain terms. A stream of lectures and publications ensued and new theories and 'solutions' were espoused, most of them hopelessly erroneous and some of them as bizarre as the translations offered by Kircher a century and a half before. In fact the hieroglyphic portion of the stone was to remain intractable for many years more. It was the study of the demotic section, recognised as the 'popular' writing mentioned in ancient Greek sources, that yielded the first positive results.

Already by the end of 1802, before the stone had had time to settle in its new home at the British Museum, two important contributions to the subject had appeared, the first by the French scholar Sylvestre de Sacy (1758–1832), the second by the Swedish diplomat and orientalist, de Sacy's pupil, Johan Åkerblad (1763–1819). The former had decided to concentrate on the demotic section as it was virtually complete, missing only the beginnings of a few lines, whereas the hieroglyphic section was incomplete and was, in any case, a less-promising proposition since 'the hieroglyphic character, being representative of ideas, not sounds, does not belong to the domain of any particular language'. De Sacy's approach to the demotic was eminently sensible. He began with the Greek proper names and attempted to isolate their demotic versions. He believed that this would enable him to identify the values of the demotic letters, which could then be used as stepping stones to further correlations. In practice the process proved to be more difficult than he had anticipated. He met with partial success in isolating the demotic groups for the names of Ptolemy and Alexander, but he found it impossible to identify the values of the individual characters.

Åkerblad, following de Sacy's method, made more substantial progress. He was able to identify in the demotic all the proper names occurring in the Greek, among them, in addition to Ptolemy and Alexander, Arsinoe, Berenice and Aelos. From the sound values thus obtained, he built up a 'demotic alphabet' of twenty-nine letters, almost half of which were actually correct. He then demonstrated that the phonetic signs used to write the names were also used to spell ordinary words, thus providing the first definite indication of the general phonetic character of the demotic script. Among several individual words, apart from names, that he correctly identified are those for 'Greek', 'Egyptian', 'temple', 'love', 'him' and 'his', all of which he was able to correlate with their Coptic equivalents. These were impressive achievements, but, ironically, Åkerblad's very success in establishing the values of so many demotic characters now led him astray. He became convinced that the script was entirely phonetic or 'alphabetic', as he called it. This belief proved an insurmountable barrier to further progress on his part.

After these early successes with the demotic, virtually nothing of value was achieved for another twelve years. Then, at the beginning of 1814, fragments of a papyrus written with 'running Egyptian characters' were submitted for study to the Englishman Thomas Young (1773–1829), a scientist of international distinction and an accomplished linguist. The study of this material aroused his interest in the Rosetta inscriptions and in the summer of that year he began to subject them to the most careful scrutiny. He began, like de Sacy and Åkerblad before, with the demotic or 'epistolographic' as it was also known. Within a few weeks Young had been able to isolate in the demotic most of the graphic groups representing individual words and to relate them to their equivalents in the Greek, but he found it difficult to go further:

> 'You tell me that I shall astonish the world if I make out the inscription. I think it on the contrary astonishing that it should not have been made out already, and that I should find the task so difficult as it appears to be ... by far the greater part of the words I have ascertained with tolerable certainty, and some of the

most interesting without the shadow of a doubt; but I can read very few of them alphabetically, except the proper names which Åkerblad had read before . . .'

An important observation was soon to follow, however:

> 'after having completed this analysis of the hieroglyphic inscription, I observed that the epistolographic characters of the Egyptian inscription, which expressed the words God, Immortal, Vulcan, Priests, Diadem, Thirty, and some others, had a striking resemblance to the corresponding hieroglyphs; and since none of these characters could be reconciled, without inconceivable violence, to the forms of any imaginable alphabet, I could scarcely doubt that they were imitations of the hieroglyphics, adopted as monograms or verbal characters, and mixed with the letters of the alphabet.'

These are the first intimations of two crucially important points: firstly that demotic was not a wholly separate script from hieroglyphic; secondly that the Egyptian system was a mix of different types of character.

In the year or so following, Young spread his researches beyond the Rosetta texts, drawing also on other material, an increasing amount of which was now becoming available. Particularly useful for him were the inscriptions newly published in the volumes of the *Description de l'Égypte* (the scholarly fruits of the Napoleonic expedition) and some unpublished papyri, 'funeral rolls', recently brought from Egypt and placed at his disposal. His eye for significant detail is revealed by his observation that the hieroglyphic group , which he commonly found attached to what were evidently personal names in the funerary papyri, was in fact a 'female termination', a sound conclusion that was to be of considerable value at a later stage of the decipherment. Even more significantly, by the judicious comparison of parallel texts occurring in the funerary documents, he was able to confirm the relationship of the various Egyptian scripts by tracing the 'degradation from the *sacred* character, through the *hieratic*, into the *epistolographic*, or common running hand of the country'. This conclusion led him on directly to what was to be his single most important contribution to the process of decipherment: the partial subversion of the great myth that the hieroglyphic script was entirely 'symbolic'. Turning back again to the Rosetta texts, he now quickly established the equivalence of many of the demotic and hieroglyphic signs. One of the outcomes of this process was the firm identification of the only personal name that occurs in the hieroglyphic section, that of King Ptolemy. Since the demotic expressed the name phonetically, it was logical to conclude, in Young's view, that the hieroglyphic equivalent did so also.

The name of Ptolemy occurs six times in the hieroglyphic section, three in a short cartouche and three in a longer one:

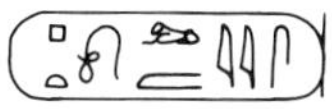

'Ptolemaios'

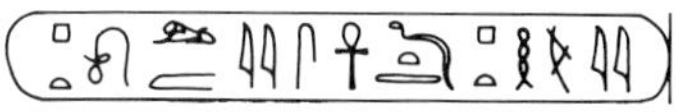

'Ptolemaios, may he live for ever beloved of Ptah'

Deducing that the shorter contained the name Ptolemy alone, while the longer contained the name plus title, Young conjectured the phonetic values of the name signs to be as follows:

Hieroglyph	Young Value	Correct Value
	p	p
	t	t
	'not essentially necessary'	o

Hieroglyph	Young Value	Correct Value
	lo or ole	l
	ma or simply m	m
	i	i or y
	osh or os	s

He followed this with a similar analysis of the name of the Ptolemaic queen, Berenice, which he had isolated, somewhat fortuitously, on a copy of an inscription from the temple of Karnak at Thebes:

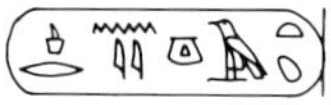

Hieroglyph	Young Value	Correct Value
	bir	b
	e	r
	n	n
	i	i
	'superfluous'	k
	ke or ken	a
	'feminine termination'	female determinative

These two analyses, with the hieroglyphs treated as phonograms (and four or five of them quite correctly identified), represent an enormous step forward conceptually. The door was now open at last to a real understanding of the largely phonetic nature of the hieroglyphic script. Sadly, at the very threshold, Young's progress came to an abrupt halt. The old myth still exercised a potent influence. Young was convinced that the phonetic principle could only be of limited validity, that the 'hieroglyphic alphabet' was a 'mode of expressing sounds in some particular cases, and not as having been universally employed where sounds were required'. In other words, the hieroglyphs were mostly symbolic; only in special cases, such as in the rendering of foreign names, were they used to represent sounds. Drawing on an analogy from Chinese, he viewed the cartouche surrounding the royal name as a mark denoting that this special process was in operation:

> 'it is extremely interesting to trace some of the steps by which alphabetic writing seems to have arisen out of hieroglyphical; a process which may indeed be in some measure illustrated by the manner in which the modern Chinese express a foreign combination of sounds, the characters being rendered simply 'phonetic' by an appropriate mark, instead of retaining their natural signification; and this mark, in some modern printed books, approaching very near to the ring surrounding the hieroglyphic names.'

The results of Young's researches, of four years' duration in all, were published by him in 1819 in a splendid article entitled 'Egypt' for the *Supplement to the fourth edition of the Encyclopaedia Britannica*. In the years following he continued to work, with intermittent success, on the problems of the hieroglyphs, but he entirely failed to capitalise on his own initial breakthrough. The prize of final decipherment was to fall to another scholar, Young's contemporary and rival, the brilliant young Frenchman, Jean-François Champollion (1790–1832).

The latter's route to the decipherment was also via the name of Ptolemy, the identity of

40 *Right* Jean-François Champollion
(1790–1832). Portrait by Coignet,
1831. Musée du Louvre, Paris.

41 *Below* A plate from Champollion's
Lettre à M. Dacier, published in
1822. Listed are the various demotic
and hieroglyphic signs which form
the Egyptian 'phonetic alphabet'
together with their Greek equivalents.
At the bottom enclosed in a cartouche
is Champollion's name written by
him in demotic.

Pl. IV.

Tableau des Signes Phonétiques
des écritures hiéroglyphique et Démotique des anciens Egyptiens

Lettres Grecques	Signes Démotiques	Signes Hiéroglyphiques
A		
B		
Γ		
Δ		
E		
Z		
H		
Θ		
I		
K		
Λ		
M		
N		
Ξ		
O		
Π		
P		
Σ		
T		
Υ		
Φ		
Ψ		
X		
Ω		
TO ou		

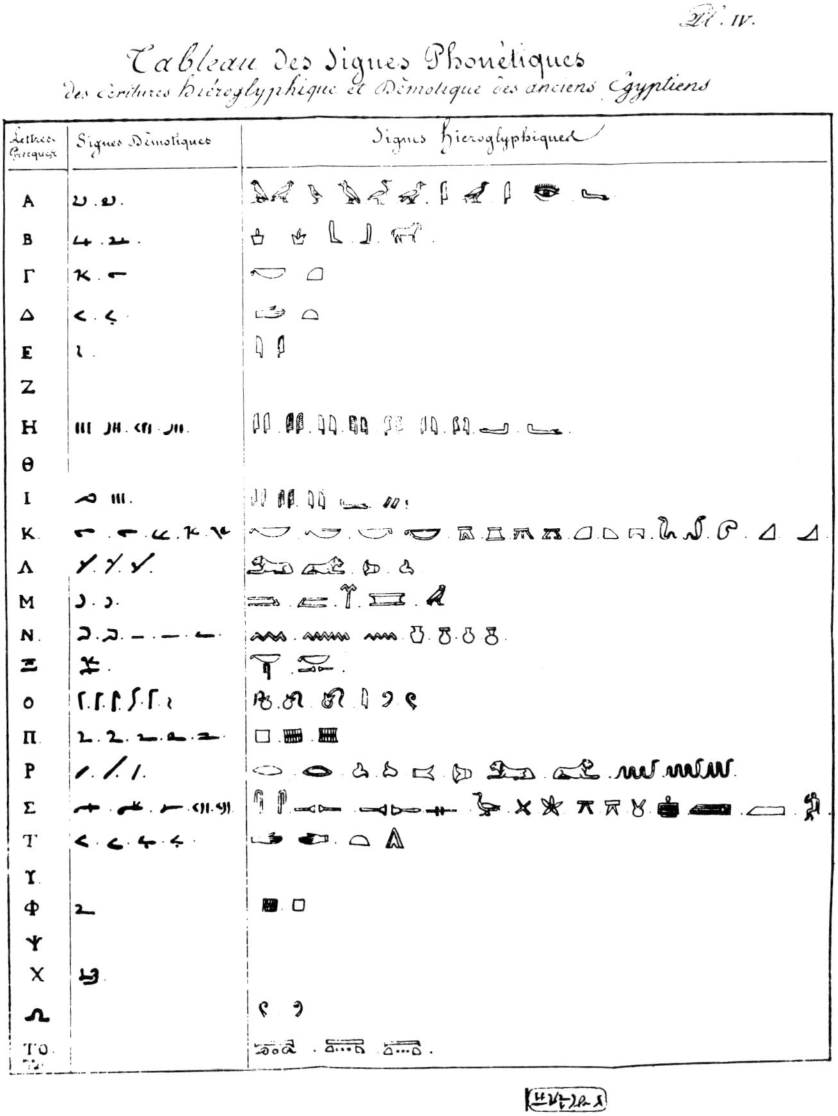

which he appears to have determined by a similar process of deduction to that of Young. To what extent, if any, Champollion's initial discoveries were dependent on Young's work has long been a matter of dispute. Champollion's famous paper on the phonetic nature of the hieroglyphs, *Lettre à M. Dacier relative à l'alphabet des hiéroglyphes phonétiques*, appeared in 1822, three years after Young's article 'Egypt'. Whether or not Champollion learned anything from Young, it is beyond dispute that he rapidly overtook him. Young's results, though they pointed in the right direction, were limited and inconclusive. Champollion was the first to *prove*, by systematic analysis of the available evidence, that the hieroglyphic script operated on the phonetic principle, and to build on this effectively. Champollion realised that to make real progress it was necessary somehow to isolate a pair of already known names having several hieroglyphs in common. These would act as an independent check on each other and would provide a firm basis for further identifications. In early 1822, by a happy chance, a copy of another bilingual inscription containing just such a pair of names came into his hands.

In 1819 the English traveller, W. J. Bankes, had transported back from Egypt to his home in Kingston Lacy, Dorset, an obelisk and its base block, which had once stood in the temple of Philae near Aswan. On the base was a Greek inscription mentioning two royal names, Ptolemy and Cleopatra, while on the obelisk itself was a hieroglyphic text including two different cartouches. Bankes inferred from the Greek that the cartouches contained the names of Ptolemy and Cleopatra and noted that the hieroglyphs in one corresponded exactly to those in the cartouche on the Rosetta Stone identified as Ptolemy by Young. In 1821 Bankes had a lithograph made of both the Greek and hieroglyphic texts, copies of which, annotated by Bankes with the suggested identifications of the names, were widely distributed. For Champollion the receipt of one of these copies was, in the words of one commentator, 'the moment which ... turned bewildering investigation into brilliant and continuous decipherment'.

Omitting the epithets accompanying the name of Ptolemy and the signs representing the 'female termination' in the other, the cartouches on the Bankes' obelisk read so:

Ptolemaios   Cleopatra

Champollion identified the values of the individual signs as follows:

□	= p		△	= c
○	= t			= l
	= o			= e
	= l			= o
	= m		□	= p
	= e			= a
	= s			= t
				= r
				= a

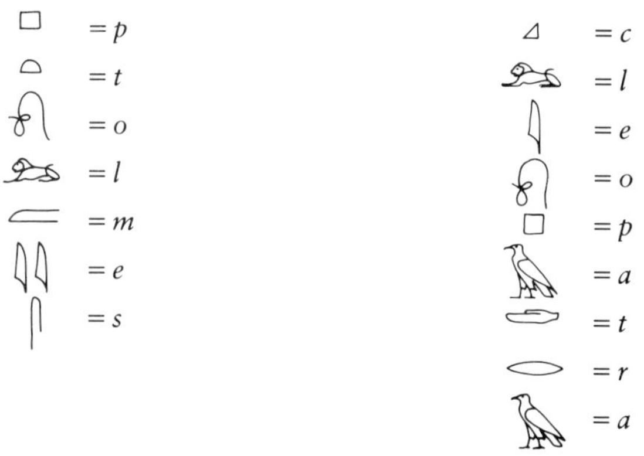

There was an encouraging degree of correspondence between the signs which occurred in both names. Only the ○ and ▭ did not correlate but for this Champollion had a ready explanation. He deduced correctly that the two signs were actually 'homophones' – separate signs that could represent the same value, here a *t*.

Champollion knew that if these identifications were correct it should be possible to apply the values gained from the names of Ptolemy and Cleopatra to other cartouches and to produce further recognisable names. This he now proceeded to do, beginning with the cartouche: 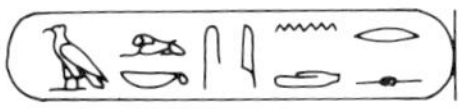

From the known values the following elements could be identified:

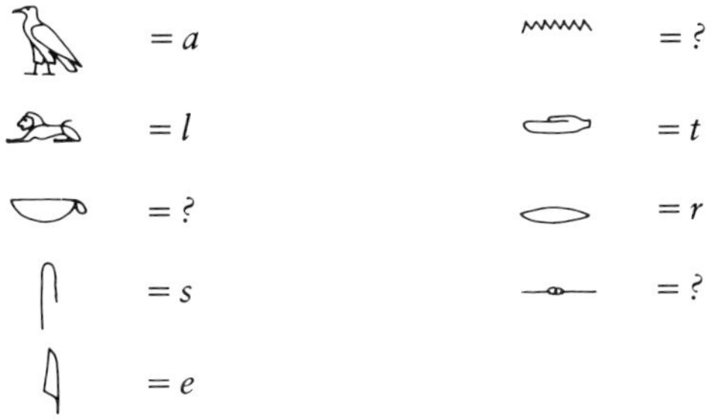

When the range of possible names was considered, it was not difficult to fill the gaps with *k*, *n*, and *s* to yield the name *alksentrs* = Greek Alexandros (Alexander), with ,  identified as *k*, *n* and *s* respectively, the first and last understood as homophones for  and . By the extension of this method there quickly followed further identifications, including the name of Queen Berenice (confirming and correcting Young's suggestions) and the names and titles of several Roman emperors:

Berenice

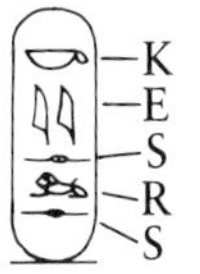

Caesar

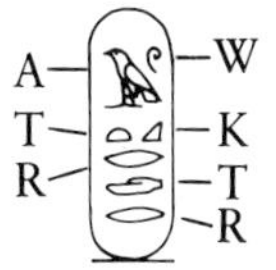

Autocrator

It seems that during at least the initial stages of the decipherment Champollion had believed, like Young, that the phonetic system operated only for the expression of foreign names and elements of the Graeco-Roman Period. It was to these that his *Lettre à M. Dacier*, published in late 1822, was largely devoted. At the end of the *Lettre*, however, he announced an entirely new and astonishing discovery: the phonetic system was of wider application and could be extended back into earlier times. The final breakthrough had been achieved.

It appears that in September 1822 Champollion had received copies of various reliefs and inscriptions from Egyptian temples. One of them, from the temple of Abu Simbel in Nubia, contained cartouches enclosing a name repeated in a variety of ways but in its simplest form as . The last two signs were familiar to him from the cartouches of the Graeco-Roman rulers as bearing the phonetic value *s*. But what of the first two signs? Champollion had an excellent knowledge of Coptic and here it came fully into play. The first hieroglyph appeared to represent the sun, for which the Coptic word was ⲣⲏ (rē). Supplying this value for the first hieroglyph produced the sequence

Re + ? + *s* + *s*. There immediately sprung to Champollion's mind the combination *Re* + *m* + *s* + *s* yielding the well-known name Rameses or Ramesses, identified as a king of the Nineteenth Dynasty in the history (written in Greek) of the Ptolemaic historian, Manetho. By this analysis, the sign 𓄟 should logically be accorded the value *m*. More evidence was at hand. A second sheet of drawings included the cartouche (𓅝𓄟𓋴). Here again was the group 𓄟𓋴 already conjectured to be *m* + *s*, in this case preceded by a hieroglyph that Champollion recognised as the picture of an ibis, known to be the symbol of the god Thoth. Surely the name was none other than Thoth-mes, the Tuthmosis of Manetho's Eighteenth Dynasty. For confirmation of the value of 𓄟 Champollion was able to turn to the Rosetta Stone, where the sign occurs, again in conjunction with 𓋴, as part of a group corresponding to the Greek *genethlia*, 'birth day', which at once suggested to Champollion the Coptic word for 'give birth', ⲙⲓⲥⲉ (mīse). It should be noted that Champollion was actually in error in interpreting 𓄟 as having the value *m*. It does, in fact, have the value *ms*, being a biconsonantal sign to which 𓋴 had been added as a phonetic complement. At this stage, understandably, Champollion was unaware of the possibility of multiconsonantal signs. Fortunately the error was not crucial.

Champollion published these and many other subsequent discoveries in his *Précis du système hiéroglyphique* (1824), a work in which he conclusively demonstrated that the phonetic principle, far from being of limited application, was, as he called it, the 'soul' of the entire writing system. For the first time the true relationship between the semograms and the phonograms, including the function of the determinative, was revealed. In addition a huge quantity of new data was presented and identified – royal, private and divine names, titles and epithets, as well as ordinary vocabulary. Furthermore there was grammatical analysis and translation of phrases and sentences. Inevitably there were mistakes, but the fundamental approach was absolutely sound. With the appearance of the *Précis*, the ancient myth of the hieroglyphs was finally laid to rest and the science of Egyptology was born.

6
Borrowings

No account of the hieroglyphic script would be complete without some consideration of its contribution to the writing of languages other than Egyptian. The other great writing system of the ancient Near East, cuneiform, was adapted through the course of three millennia to write a large variety of languages. By comparison the Egyptian contribution was small but was not completely insignificant. Some scholars believe that the example of Egyptian hieroglyphs may well have stimulated the development of Cretan and Hittite 'hieroglyphs' in the first half of the second millennium BC. More certainly, in the case of two other scripts – Protosinaitic and Meroïtic – there was the direct borrowing of Egyptian signs.

Protosinaitic

Protosinaitic is a script that was initially noted in various localities in the Sinai peninsula, hence its name. Serious attention was first drawn to it in 1906 by the British archaeologist, Flinders Petrie (1853–1942), following his expedition to Sinai where he explored the sites of the turquoise mines worked anciently by the Egyptians. The most important of these sites, Serabit el-Khadim, bore the remains of a temple dedicated to Hathor, the chief goddess of the Sinai mining area. It was here that Petrie made his most substantial discoveries, including a large number of inscriptions, many dedicated to Hathor, by the personnel of the expeditions. The vast majority were written in Egyptian, but some of the monuments bore texts in a script (there were eleven such texts in all) that contained 'a mixture of Egyptian hieroglyphs ... though not a word of regular Egyptian could be read'. One of these, a sphinx-statuette, is particularly interesting in that it bears 42
texts written both in ordinary Egyptian script and in the Sinaitic script. The Egyptian is inscribed between the paws and on the right shoulder, where it reads 'beloved of Hathor,

42 Sandstone sphinx statuette with inscriptions in Egyptian hieroglyphs and in Protosinaitic. Second Intermediate Period. Serabit el-Khadim. L. 23.7 cm. BM 41748.

43 Sphinx statuette, detail. Part of the Protosinaitic inscription on the left side including the group identified as 'Balat'.

mistress of turquoise', the Sinaitic is written on both the right and left sides on the upper surfaces of the pedestal. Petrie was unable to offer any suggestions as to the reading of the script but he did make some perceptive observations. He noted, for example, that in view of the limited number of signs the new script was likely to be alphabetic and that in view of the context it probably represented the Semitic language of the Asiatic workers on the staff of the expeditions. Petrie dated the material to the middle of the Eighteenth Dynasty but in this he was probably wrong. The sculptural style of the sphinx and of some of the other pieces indicates an earlier date, in all likelihood the late Middle Kingdom or Second Intermediate Period.

Table 2 The Sinaitic script appears to consist of at least twenty-three separate signs, the forms of nearly half of which are clearly borrowed from Egyptian. Like the hieroglyphs the signs are arranged either in columns or in horizontal lines but they seem generally to read from left to right. There appears to have been no strict rule as to which direction the individual signs should face, though within a single text the direction is consistent. The first breakthrough in deciphering the system was made in 1916 by the English scholar, A. H. (later Sir Alan) Gardiner (1879–1963). He noticed that a number of the signs depicted objects or things, the Semitic names for which correspond to the names of letters in the later Phoenician/Canaanite alphabet. Gardiner was led to the conclusion that the linear forms of the latter were actually derived from the Sinaitic 'pictograms' and showed that the transition in form from one to the other was in many cases traceable without undue difficulty. Moreover in assigning to the Sinai pictograms the phonetic values of their alphabetic descendants he was able

43 to read the commonly occurring group  as *bʿlt*, 'Balat'. This makes very good sense in the context, since Balat is the name of a Semitic goddess closely identified with Hathor, whose name, in addition, occurs written in Egyptian hieroglyphs, on the sphinx that is one of the monuments bearing the group in question. Gardiner was unable to make further progress with the material at hand, but the fact that by a process of logical deduction, unforced by prejudice, the Sinai texts had been made to yield perhaps the one name most likely to occur in the area has been regarded as a powerful factor in favour of his interpretation of the script.

Since Gardiner's initial contribution, a great deal of scholarly work has been carried out on Protosinaitic. The stock of available texts has more than trebled and these now include inscriptions from places other than Sinai. Unfortunately the texts are invariably short and often crudely executed. Progress in further understanding has been slow, and has been limited on the whole to small gains in vocabulary. A complete decipherment of the script published in 1966 by the American scholar W. F. Albright (1891–1971) has

Table 2: Protosinaitic signs and Egyptian prototypes (Protosinaitic forms after Albright).

not received general acceptance. Probably the most important development has been the realisation that the Sinaitic texts are not an isolated group. Inscriptions written in what appear to be basically the same script have been identified in various localities in Palestine. Some are roughly contemporary with the Sinaitic texts, others are later. The corpus as a whole, including the Sinai material, is now referred to by some scholars as Proto-Canaanite.

That the system represents an early stage in the history of the alphabet seems very feasible. Recent studies in the palaeography of the texts have tended to confirm its suggested relationship with the later Canaanite or Phoenician alphabet, though a link is not demonstrable in the case of every individual sign. The system is not strictly 'alphabetic' in the proper sense but is really an 'economical syllabary' in which each sign stands for a consonant + any vowel. In its creation the Egyptian writing system is thought to have been influential, supplying not only the actual sign-forms, or at least some of them, but also providing with its uniconsonantal signs a partial model for just such a restricted signary. If this view is correct (and it is not accepted by all scholars), it has an interesting implication. Since the Canaanite/Phoenician syllabary formed the basis of the Greek alphabet, and the Greek in turn of the Latin, it means, in the words of Gardiner, that 'the hieroglyphs live on, though in transmuted form, within our own alphabet'.

Table 3

Egyptian	Protosinaitic	Phoenician	Early Greek	Greek	Latin
			Λ	A	A
				B	B
			1	Γ	G
				E	E
				k	K
				M	M
				N	N
		o	o	O	O
				P	R
	+	×	T	T	T
		W		Σ	S

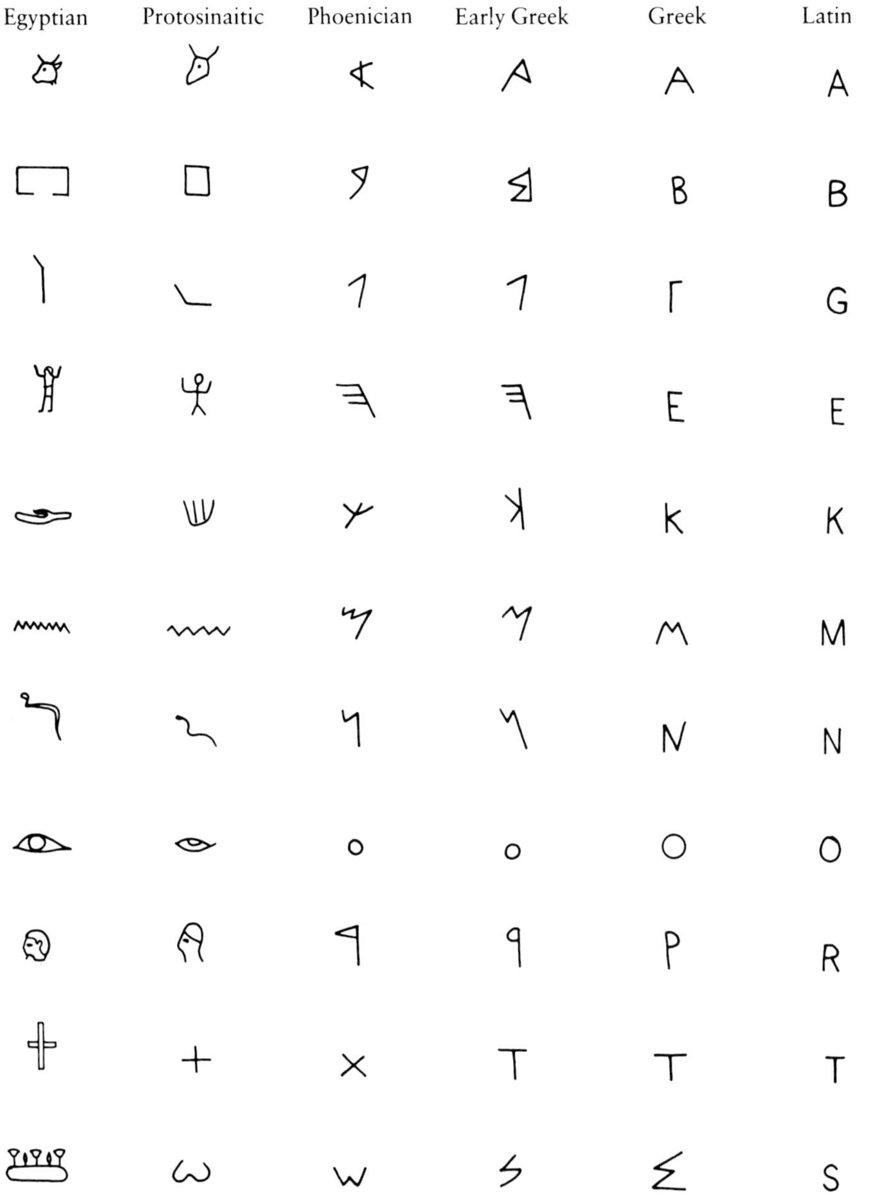

Table 3: From hieroglyphic sign to alphabetic letter.

Meroïtic

Meroïtic was the native language of a great African civilisation, known to the Egyptians as the 'Kingdom of Kush', which during the later periods of Egyptian history had its capital at Meroë (modern Begrawiya in the Sudan).

The language was first recorded in writing in the second century BC in an 'alphabetic' script consisting of twenty-three symbols, most of which were borrowed or at least derived from Egyptian writing. The system is quite different from Egyptian. Every sign has a phonetic value, and vowels as well as consonants are represented. There is also a special symbol for marking the division between words. The script has two forms, hieroglyphic and cursive. Hieroglyphic inscriptions are normally written in columns, cursive in horizontal lines reading from right to left. Unlike Egyptian the individual signs read in the direction which the figures face. Table 4

Although it looks alphabetic, Meroïtic is in fact a syllabic system. A 'consonantal' sign does not represent a single consonant but a consonant plus the vowel a, except when it is followed by one of the signs i, o and e. The special sign for the vowel a is used only at the beginning of words. There are separate signs for the combinations n + e, s + e, t + e, and t + o. In addition the sign for e has two uses: not only does it represent the vowel e, but it can also denote the lack of a vowel following a consonant.

The corpus of known Meroïtic inscriptions is much larger than that of Protosinaitic but is still relatively small. To date fewer than 1,000 individual texts have been properly

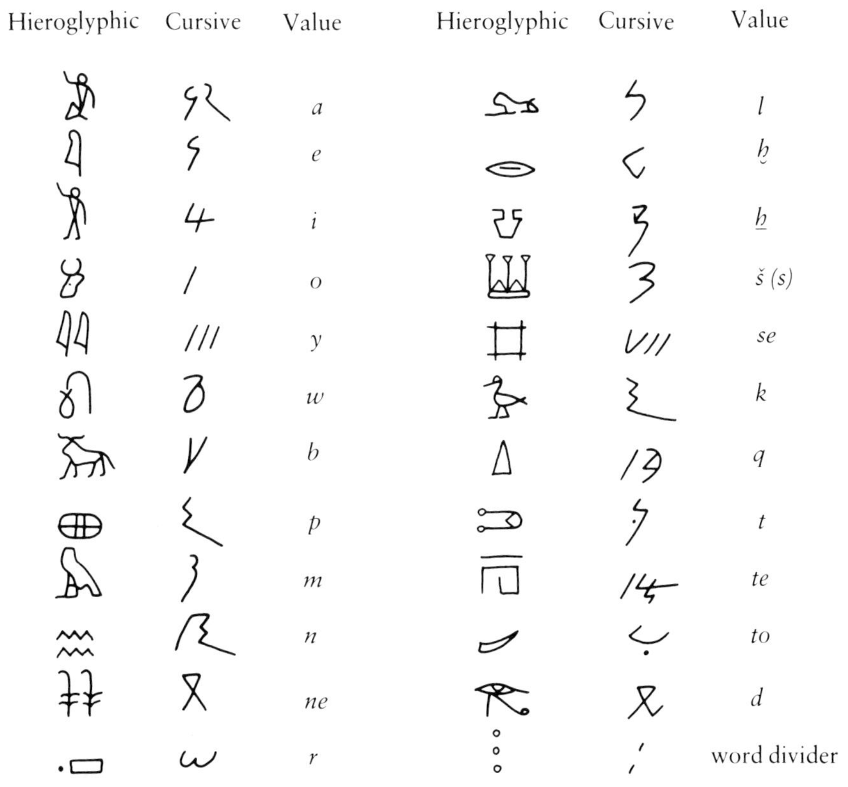
Hieroglyphic
Cursive
Value
Hieroglyphic
Cursive
Value
a
e
i
o
y
w
b
p
m
n
ne
r
l
ḫ
ẖ
š (s)
se
k
q
t
te
to
d
word divider

Table 4: Meroïtic syllabary (after Hintze).

documented, though this total is increasing steadily. They have been found throughout the length of the Sudanese and Nubian Nile valley from Philae in the north to Naqa near Khartoum in the south and occur in a wide range of contexts – on temple walls, shrines, altars, offering tables, stelae, statues, pottery vessels, ostraca, papyri, and in the form of rock-graffiti. Inscriptions in the hieroglyphic script are comparatively rare and are largely confined to royal and divine 'prestige' contexts. Cursive is much more common. It was the 'everyday' script and gradually supplanted its ornamental companion. The earliest dated text in Meroïtic is a hieroglyphic temple inscription of Queen Shanakdakhete (*c.* 180–170 BC). There is no evidence for its use, in either form, after the fifth century AD.

The fundamental work on Meroïtic was carried out by the British Egyptologist, Francis Llewellyn Griffith (1862–1934), in the first decade or so of this century. By a detailed comparison of parallel funerary formulae occurring on offering tables and stelae, Griffith was able to determine the size of the Meroïtic syllabary, to prove the correlation between the hieroglyphic and cursive scripts, and to show in which direction the signs were to be read. He then went on to establish the phonetic values of the signs.
44 The key to this achievement was an inscription carved on the base of a sacred boat from the temple of Ban Naqa in the Sudan, now in the Berlin Museum. Included in this inscription are the cartouches of two rulers of Meroë, a king and a queen, Natakemeni and Amanitere, who were dedicators of the monument. The vital point is that the names are written in both Meroïtic and Egyptian hieroglyphs. Since the phonetic values of the Egyptian signs were known, it was possible for Griffith to deduce the values of the Meroïtic equivalents. The values of eight separate signs, over one third of the complete syllabary, were thus more or less correctly established from this one inscription. By cleverly isolating in other Meroïtic texts various well-known names such as those of the gods Osiris and Isis and place names like Philae, Griffith quickly established the values of the remaining signs. The system established by Griffith has since been refined and modified in points of detail, most notably by the German scholar Fritz Hintze, but it is agreed to have been essentially correct.

This success in transliterating the scripts has not, unfortunately, been followed by an equivalent progress in understanding the language which they write. Some words and phrases have been made out with reasonable certainty and some grammatical constructions tentatively identified, but the meaning of the vast majority of inscriptions remains obscure. The task of deciphering the language would be considerably aided if a link between Meroïtic and some other known language could be established. This has yet to be achieved. Meroïtic does not apparently belong to the Afro-Asiatic family and attempts to place it within one of the African groups of languages have hitherto proved inconclusive. It seems likely that really significant progress will have to await the discovery of a bilingual text, another 'Rosetta Stone', written in Meroïtic and some other known language, like Egyptian or Greek.

44 Stand from Ban Naga with inscriptions in Egyptian and Meroïtic hieroglyphs. 0-AD 20. H. 1.18 m. East Berlin, 7261.

Bibliography

Albright, William Foxwell, *The Proto-Sinaitic Inscriptions and their Decipherment*, Harvard/London, 1966
Andrews, Carol, *The Rosetta Stone*, London, 1981
Assmann, Aleida and Jan, and Christof Hardmeier (eds), *Schrift und Gedächtnis. Beiträge zur Archäologie der literarischen Kommunikation*, Munich, 1983
Baines, John, 'Literacy and Ancient Egyptian Society', *Man* 18, 1983, pp. 572–99
Baines, John R., 'Schreiben' in Wolfgang Helck and Wolfhart Westendorf (eds), *Lexikon der Ägyptologie*, V, Wiesbaden, 1984, cols 693–8
Bynon, James and Theodora (eds), *Hamito-Semitica. Proceedings of a Colloquium held by the Historical Section of the Linguistics Association (Great Britain) at the School of Oriental and African Studies, University of London, on the 18th, 19th and 20th of March 1970*, The Hague, 1975
Callender, John B., *Middle Egyptian*, Malibu, 1975
Caminos, Ricardo, and Henry G. Fischer, *Ancient Egyptian Epigraphy and Palaeography*, New York, 1976
Černý, J., *Paper and books in ancient Egypt*, London, 1952
Davies, Nina M., *Picture Writing in Ancient Egypt*, Oxford, 1958
Faulkner, Raymond O., *A Concise Dictionary of Middle Egyptian*, Oxford, 1962
Fischer, Henry George, *L'écriture et l'art de l'Égypte ancienne. Quatre leçons sur la paléographie et l'épigraphie pharaoniques*, Paris, 1986
Fischer, Henry George, *Egyptian Studies*, II. *The Orientation of Hieroglyphs*, Part 1 *Reversals*, New York, 1977
Fischer, Henry G., 'Hieroglyphen' in Wolfgang Helck and Wolfhart Westendorf (eds), *Lexikon der Ägyptologie*, II, Wiesbaden, 1977, cols 1189–99
Galeries nationales du Grand Palais, *Naissance de l'écriture. Cuneiformes et hiéroglyphes*, exh. cat., Paris, 1982
Gardiner, Alan H., 'The Egyptian Origin of the Semitic Alphabet', *The Journal of Egyptian Archaeology* 3, 1916, pp. 1–16
Gardiner, Sir Alan, *Egyptian Grammar. Being an Introduction to the Study of Hieroglyphs*, 3rd edn (rev.), Oxford, 1957
Gaur, Albertine, *A History of Writing*, London, 1984
Gelb, I. J., *A Study of Writing. A discussion of the general principles governing the use and evolution of writing*, rev. edn, Chicago, 1963
Griffith, F. L., *Meroitic Inscriptions*, Parts I and II, London, 1911 and 1912
Harris, J. R. (ed.), *The Legacy of Egypt*, 2nd edn, Oxford, 1971
Harris, Roy, *The Origin of Writing*, London, 1986
Hawkins, J. D., 'The origin and dissemination of writing in western Asia' in P. R. S. Moorey (ed.), *The Origins of Civilization*, Oxford, 1979, pp. 128–66
Henderson, Leslie, *Orthography and Word Recognition in Reading*, London, 1982
Hintze, Fritz, 'The Meroitic Period' in *Africa in Antiquity. The Arts of Ancient Nubia and the Sudan* I. *The Essays*, Brooklyn Museum exh. cat., Brooklyn, 1978, pp. 89–105
Hodge, Carleton T. (ed.), *Afroasiatic. A Survey*, The Hague, 1971
Iversen, Erik, *The Myth of Egypt and its Hieroglyphs in European Tradition*, Copenhagen, 1961
Lewis, Naphtali, *Papyrus in Classical Antiquity*, Oxford, 1974
Lichtheim, M., *Ancient Egyptian Literature*, 3 vols, California, 1973–80
Meltzer, E. S., 'Remarks on ancient Egyptian writing with emphasis on its mnemonic aspects' in Paul A. Kolers, Merald E. Wrolstad and Herman Bouma (eds), *Processing of Visible Language* 2, New York/London, 1980
Millard, A. R., 'The Infancy of the Alphabet', *World Archaeology*, 17, no. 3, 1986, pp. 390–8
Pope, Maurice, *The Story of Decipherment from Egyptian hieroglyphic to Linear B*, London, 1975
Quaegebeur, J., 'De la préhistoire de l'écriture Copte', *Orientalia Lovaniensia Periodica* 13, Leuven, 1982, pp. 125–36
Ray, John D., 'The Emergence of Writing in Egypt', *World Archaeology* 17, no. 3, 1986, pp. 307–16
Sampson, Geoffrey, *Writing Systems. A linguistic introduction*, London, 1985
Schäfer, Heinrich, *Principles of Egyptian Art*, ed., with an epilogue, by Emma Brunner-Traut; trans. and ed., with an introduction, by John Baines, Oxford, 1974
Shinnie, P. L., *Meroe: a civilization of the Sudan*, London, 1967
Schenkel, Wolfgang, 'Schrift' in Wolfgang Helck and Wolfhart Westendorf (eds), *Lexikon der Ägyptologie*, V, Wiesbaden, 1984, cols 713–35
Schenkel, Wolfgang, 'The structure of hieroglyphic script', *Royal Anthropological Institute News*, 15, 1976, pp. 4–7
Williams, R. J., 'Scribal training in ancient Egypt', *Journal of the American Oriental Society* 92, 1972, pp. 214–21

Index